In Search of Language

Enhancing Language Acquisition in the Classroom

John De Mado

Dear Christina —
Best regards . . .
John DeMado

In Search of Language

ISBN: 978-1-947758-07-0

Book design and production by:
Indie Author Books
12 High Street, Thomaston, Maine 04861
www.indieauthorbooks.com

DEDICATION

This book is dedicated to the thousands of language teachers I have had the pleasure of meeting over the course of decades.

> "Come to the edge, he said.
> They said: We are afraid.
> Come to the edge, he said.
> They came.
> He pushed them and they flew."
>
> —Guillaume Apollinaire

Table of Contents

Prologue

The Airport Interlude

The Chinese man presented himself to the employee in the 'Airport Information' booth. He had just flown halfway around the world, anticipating an arrival in Cincinnati; or, at the very least, in Ohio. Instead, he found himself somewhere in Northern Kentucky.

Slowly looking up from his Louis Lamour paperback novel, the 'Airport Information' employee peered over his glasses at the beleaguered traveler and fired out the following perfunctory phrase in a most recognizable, indigenous Northern Kentucky accent… "Hep 'ya?"

Waiting as well at the booth for my chauffeur (*French for van driver*), I could not help but think to myself that the ensuing exchange between the Chinese national and the airport employee was going to be memorable!

It most certainly was…

Miraculously enough, the Chinese man understood the question posed by the indigenous Northern Kentucky type. *This gave me cause to believe that perhaps there are CDs floating about Beijing for practicing indigenous Northern Kentucky speech patterns.*

As is the custom, the Chinese man, once acknowledged, graciously bowed to the 'Airport Information' employee and said in his best English, *"I need mop…"*

The airport employee's eyes narrowed. Slowly leaning forward, he said *"What the heck 'ya need a mop for?"*

Sensing that he might not have delivered his intended message, the Chinese man regrouped and tried to renegotiate his phrase. *"I need mop airport… I need mop airport…"*

Now, overtly irritated by what he found to be a complete waste of his expert time and talents, the indigenous Northern Kentucky type brusquely shot back *"Mop the airport? What the heck 'ya need to mop the airport for?"*

That's when I jumped into the exchange. *"He doesn't need a* ***mop****!"* I said in exasperation. *"He needs a* ***map****! Does he look like he mops airports for a living? An international airport mopper, perhaps? And today is your day?... Why would he fly all the way from China to mop your airport? And why would he ask YOU for a mop? Do you normally stock mops in your information booth?"*

In retrospect, I should have given the 'Airport Information' employee a quick lesson in 'negotiation of meaning'. I should have said *"What are the things that this man might possibly need? A mip? A mep? How about a mup? The only choices left are map and mop. And, given the context, why would someone come to an information booth for a mop?"*

This airport scene simply underscores what I have always known intuitively about people who are multilingual... They simply make better listeners than monolinguals because they are willing to negotiate meaning and are well practiced in the art. Multilinguals maintain a subset of hard-earned skills that help them to seek comprehensible input by focusing on extra-linguistic cues, such as considering the general context, observing the particular body language, hand gestures, facial expressions and by intuiting the message.

Adults who are unable to read, write or calculate normally spend a lifetime at covert activity designed to disguise their disability. Yet, monolingual Americans laugh uproariously as they relate the various horrors that they endured in the World Language classroom. And their story always ends with the same summation; one which ultimately provides cradle-to-grave coverage for monolingualism; *"When I was in school, I wasn't smart enough... And now, I'm too old."*

Monolingualism is not only a personal disadvantage. It is a disability as well. That's right... a disability. It stands to reason that if functioning in *more* than one language is an ability, as so many monolinguals contend, it follows that anything less is a disability.

We Americans seem convinced that we have fallen victim to a certain genetic stamping which dooms us to a life of monolingualism; some sort of natural disability that afflicts us, keeping multilingualism outside the scope of the American mind. *"We just can't do it!"*

To my way of thinking, this condition is due neither to predetermination nor relative geographic isolation nor depletion of the ozone layer. It is **pedogenic** in nature… or instructionally induced. American attitudes toward language acquisition and related instructional methods, rooted in nineteenth century beliefs and mythologies, have created an historic *delivery system* which has no option but to produce the 'linguistic and cultural cyclops' for which our nation has so long been noted.

Chapter 1

The Delivery System

In excess of a century ago, the two most commonly taught languages other than English in the United States were Latin and Classical Greek. Other than reading the great writers and subsequently writing about what was read, study of these languages held little, if any, opportunity for oral communication. Despite this fact, involvement in such an endeavor was justified by the notion that more literate students would be rendered. Minds would be disciplined. It was part of being educated and refined. As Alice Omaggio-Hadley states, "The learning of Latin and Greek had been justified as an intellectually stimulating, disciplined activity in which the mind could be trained through the logical analysis of language." (Omaggio-Hadley, 1986, p.22)

Thus, from inception, the delivery system for language study in the United States was designed more to underscore 'exclusivity' than it ever was intended to include the vast majority of students. It was assumed that one had to have a certain 'IQ' to be successful at languages of such gravitas. And its impact is still felt today and reflected in contemporary enrollment patterns. (See Figure 1.) I contend that the American agenda for language study has evolved very little over the years. It continues to be viewed by the public at large as little more than a mental gymnastic where only the brightest succeed. It paves the way to the college of your choice, setting up a quirky formula that equates how many years of language study a student is willing to *endure* to the competitiveness of his/her college choice. Considered as a rite of educational passage, there is little expectation for functioning. It is simply *a matter of endurance*.

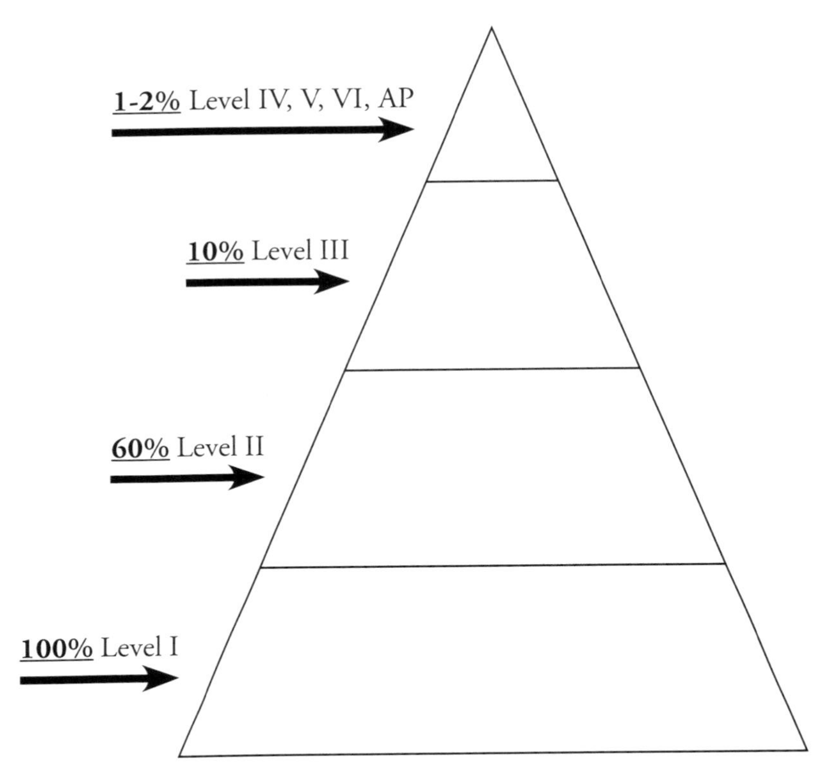

Figure 1

Figure 1 indicates that, nationally, over a four to seven year period (middle school/ high school), language classrooms standardly shed as much as 98-99% of those students originally enrolled in level I coursework. Although I realize that students may opt to specialize in other content areas, culling only 1-2% of the population demonstrates that something has gone substantially awry. When one considers the extraordinary efforts expended by most language teachers to motivate students, the enrollment figures simply do not equate.

Not only are the numbers severely reduced as we scale the 'language pyramid', but the diversity of the student population changes radically as well. Ask first level teachers to describe the students enrolled in their novice level classes and they will respond *"Honey… I've got 'em all!"* From the one who sits in the 'front row' and, should you sneeze, wants you to repeat it just in case it's on the AP exam four years hence… To those who can't remember their name in the second language. The stark truth remains, however, that at the end of the four to seven year sequence, most everyone has fled our ranks with the exception of the archetypical 'front row' student'.

The implications of these demographics are quite evident. If one were to view Figure 1 as our 'delivery system', then it becomes abundantly apparent that the one we have in place is not even remotely 'inclusionary'. Quite to the contrary, it is patently 'exclusionary', bordering on being 'linguistically genocidal'. Although we might be tempted to ignore the pattern, the truth is that we end up with what we must really want. The pattern is replicated in most every school district in the USA, exposing a wide-spread, nationally-accepted practice. We systematically off-load a variety of students, even the good-natured and willing ones, in favor of those who would contend for the crown jewel of American educational politics, the AP exam.

Chapter 2

The End Product

Given the fact that we generally fashion our curricula to deliver the product just described in Chapter 1, perhaps it might be opportune to look more closely at the 'front row' student. Who is this child? And what is she/he actually capable of?

Contention #1

This student *may* very well be the least likely candidate to ever function in a second language.

The justification for my contention comes from the field of Psycholinguistics. There is good reason to believe that language is not as much a 'logical' phenomenon as it is a 'psychological' phenomenon. Accordingly, one's functionality in more than one language can quite often be contingent upon personality traits or, if you would, one's *psycholinguistic profile.*

Though the terms may vary, the general consensus among linguists is that there seems to be an intimate relationship between an individual's ability to acquire and function in a second language and his/her willingness to *risk-take, be vulnerable and to use intuition.*

As it relates to language acquisition, risk-taking might best be defined as *'a willingness on the part of the language acquirer to confront more language than he/she owns.'*

On a personal level, I am more than acquainted with this phenomenon. Although I am able to function in French, Spanish and Italian, have earned various degrees in two of the three and have worked and traveled abroad for extended periods of time, I still grow somewhat anxious when confronting the native speaker.

Dr. Stephen Krashen refers to this as the 'Affective Filter' and states that when the filter goes up, input and output of language can be impeded, if not completely blocked. What causes the rise of the filter is simply the awareness on the part of the non-native speaker that the native speaker is holding all the 'linguistic cards'. The native speaker is 'authentic', while the non-native speaker is but a mere imitation of sorts.

People that function in more than one language have learned to repress this anxiety to varying degrees by tacitly plunging into the linguistic fray and demonstrating a willingness to *'confront more language than what they own.'*

Quite often, our 'front row' student, who has been weaned on exactitude and providing accurate answers as an indication of success, is largely devoid of the capacity to take linguistic risks, thus ultimately subverting his/her ability to function in the second language.

I am recurrently reminded of the importance of linguistic *risk-taking* while observing young children. They exhibit this trait to a fault. In fact, this is squarely why they seemingly acquire their first language with such relative ease. Even when a mother intentionally truncates her language to facilitate her youngster's comprehension *(Motherese)*, it is still well beyond the linguistic capacity of the child. Yet, the child prevails… Not only negotiating the meaning, but responding as well.

Vulnerability refers to *an individual's commitment to communication, even it if it leads to less than accurate language.* It is a willingness to endure embarrassment for the broader goal of being heard and/or acquiring information. In the World Language classroom, this characteristic is largely controlled by the teacher's attitude toward error. Traditionally error has been viewed, not as a natural part of the language acquisition process, but rather as 'linguistic interference'. Consequently, we have generally *edited* our students into oblivion.

Intuition is best described as *the ability to sift for meaning* and is, in all probability, the most prized of the three. Language, at best, is ambiguous and, to large degree, inadequate for human needs. It is a sloppy affair, rife with potential for miscommunication. This is why war, random violence, domestic turmoil, divorce, etc. continue to exist in our world. They all should be avoidable through the use of language. But, alas, they are not... But, it is all that we have. Even in optimal situations, we can easily misunderstand one another. I believe that we *intuit* messages from one another. In other words, each of us makes his/her best guess as to what someone else is saying or writing.

The 'front row' student is virtually devoid of these three capacities for one specific reason. *These skills were rarely encouraged or rewarded.* She/he has scaled to the academic heights by being accurate... Neither by taking risks, nor being vulnerable, nor using intuition. And when called upon to invent language, the deficit becomes apparent. She/he can perform the chromatic scale but there is no 'jazz' forthcoming.

Contention #2

This student relies upon an 'intelligence' that is secondary to Language Acquisition.

Howard Gardner's original Theory of Multiple Intelligences (MI Theory) advises us that there are at least 7 paths to cognition or 'intelligences' that we deploy to problem solve. His original seven include:

- verbal-linguistic intelligence
- logical-mathematical intelligence
- visual-spatial intelligence
- body-kinesthetic intelligence
- musical intelligence
- interpersonal intelligence
- intrapersonal intelligence

One would think, as we are discussing language acquisition, that the 'front row' student might exhibit a demonstrable verbal-linguistic intelligence in order to ascend to the top of the language pyramid. Quite the contrary!

Instead, logical-mathematical intelligence is really his/her problem-solving device of preference. Most language teachers would agree that as children pass up and through the higher levels of language study, the study of grammar intensifies and becomes more esoteric and discrete. Grammar study is primarily a logical-mathematical phenomenon, however. It is largely 'equational' in nature. To wit:

Feminine plural noun + adjective = Feminine plural adjective
(A + B = C)

Discrete grammar study reinforces skills such as sequencing, categorizing, arranging, classifying, agreeing… All hallmark Math skills. This is why you may have heard people proclaim recurrently over the years, *"The more World Language you take, the better you'll do on the Math part of the SATs."*

Conversely, did you ever hear anyone say, *"The more Calculus you study, the better you'll do in Italian?"* Hardly… The study of grammar appeals to the logical-mathematical mind.

Communication requires virtually all of the intelligences posited by Gardner, including logical-mathematical. To emphasize and recurrently reward just one is a disservice to the language student, is patently exclusionary and perpetuates monolingualism.

Contention #3
This student is predisposed to eventually fleeing our ranks.

Given the fact that we devote our curricula to the 'front row' student and seemingly are willing to sacrifice the remainder to produce a limited number of AP candidates, it is important to note that many of these students use their AP scores to place out of World Language in college. What have we gained as language teachers?…

Chapter 3

Mastery Versus Proficiency

Figure 2 below is designed to help you identify yourself as a World Language teacher. In referencing it, you will note two paradigms, 'two instructional paths' moving from north to south. To the left, you will note the 'Mastery' paradigm while to the right you have the 'Proficiency' paradigm.

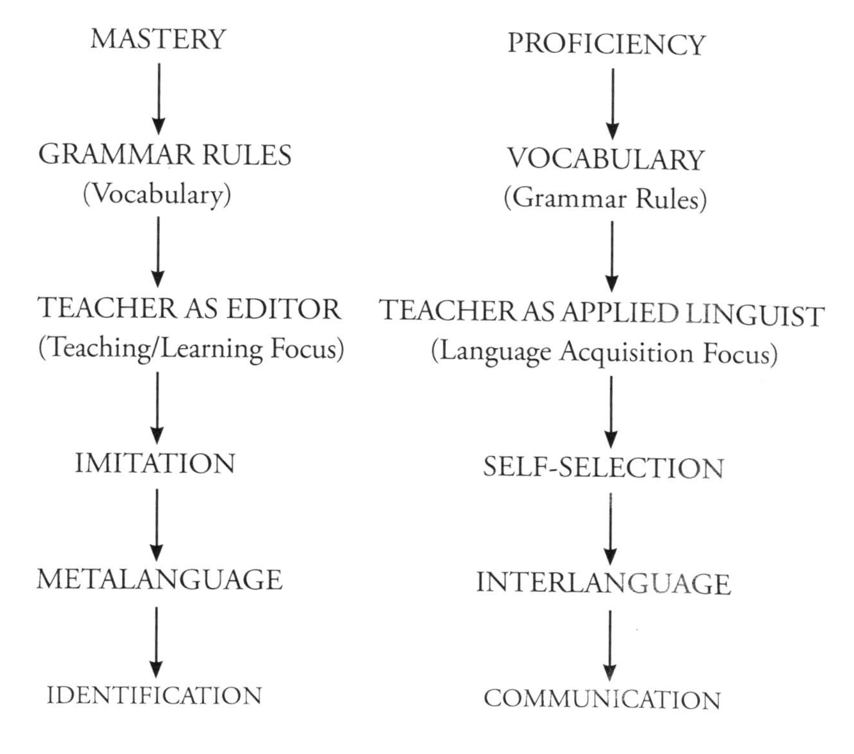

Figure 2

The terms 'Mastery' and 'Proficiency' are thought to represent the two primary language instructional approaches, although 'Proficiency' is a relative newcomer, making its US instructional debut in the late twentieth century.

It is important to note, however, that an 'approach' in not the same as a 'methodology'. An 'approach' represents the sum total of your core instructional beliefs. A 'methodology' embodies what you do in the classroom to implement your beliefs or 'approach'.

In order to more fully discuss Figure 2, I will attempt to demonstrate that:

a) Both instructional paths are quite different from one another;
b) They are mutually exclusive in that they may not be combined;
c) The results are invariable. Once either of the paradigms is implemented instructionally, certain *inevitable* results occur in the classroom.

Chapter 4

Reflections on Mastery

The mastery paradigm is the philosophical 'tierra sagrada' (holy land) from whence we all emanate as World Language teachers. The vast majority of us feel most comfortable while employing this instructional path. So, let's consider it first…

If one were to go to the dictionary for a definition of the word 'mastery', one might encounter something along the lines of … *complete ownership of, complete manipulation of, complete dominance over, complete dominion over…*

Given this interpretation, it is incumbent upon us, as World Language teachers, to now ask ourselves the critical question, *"Is it, in fact, possible to master a language?"* I would opt to say no, definitively, for two reasons:

a) Languages evolve. *(If the French can't keep the French language in check, no one can control any language…)*
b) Languages are immense. *(Go to the flagship dictionary of your own native language and humble yourself before the body of lexicon that you have not acquired. Then, consider that it will evolve and increase in next year's edition.)*

Despite the fact that mastery is, in all certainty, illogical to pursue in the World Language classroom, we still persist in our efforts as such a word is aligned with the larger notion of 'quality education.' Given that *"I don't know…"* is probably not an adequate answer when your administrator asks *"What have the kids mastered?"*, the mastery-driven teacher, even when being fully cognizant of the fact that it is impossible to master a language, is now placed in the dubious position of finding an aspect of language where the students can actually demonstrate mastery.

Resultantly, as depicted in Figure 2, the classroom falls to the study of grammar rules. Why? Because it is the only aspect of language that:

a) Does not evolve; *(Or more precisely, when it does evolve, it does so glacially…)*
b) Is not immense in volume. *(When compared to the amount of lexical items inherent to any language…)*

In other words, the discrete study of grammar is the byproduct and the inevitable result of accepting mastery as a viable instructional goal.

Note that in Figure 2, the word 'vocabulary', intentionally written in lower case letters, is listed immediately below 'GRAMMAR RULES', which is intentionally written in upper case letters. This is done to imply instructional emphasis. In the mastery-driven classroom, the vast majority of the instructional time is spent in the delivery of the grammatical syllabus. Though most of us would support the notion that vocabulary is the 'communicative' side of language, it is given short shrift in the mastery paradigm and relegated to the memorization of categorized lists. To wit:

- All the meats in the world
- All the vegetables in the world
- All the weather expressions, including *"Oh my God, it's a tsunami!" (and the student lives in Montana…)*
- All the parts of the internal combustion engine
- All the parts of the body, except the ones students *really* want to know

It all boils down to time management, with vocabulary lists becoming an expedient due to the inordinate amount of time spent on grammatical instruction.

As a result of the hyper focus on grammatical rules, which is a direct result of embracing mastery as an instructional goal, the classroom now becomes hopelessly *teacher as editor* focused, as noted above in Figure 2. Why? Quite simple, really… The World Language teacher is the only one in class who knows what she/he is talking about. The kids don't know an object pronoun from their… well… elbow.

Moreover, the World Language teacher willingly assumes the role of Editor-in-chief, correcting, modifying, seeking out and, at times, destroying student production, be it oral or written, with the laser-like stealth of a heat-seeking missile. All language flows from and through the instructor, with the classroom becoming almost completely teacher-centered.

This, of course, is a very untenable position for a World Language teacher to find him/herself in as we are supposed to be focused on the task of *language acquisition*. Don't believe me? Read the evolving American Council on the Teaching of Foreign Languages (ACTFL) research and its impact on the standards of the state in which you teach. The overriding message you will encounter states that languages are not taught. Instead, they are acquired. I want to emphasize that this fact does not diminish the role of the World Language *teacher*. It exalts it. It is crucial, however, that the teacher finally conclude that *what she/he is attempting to teach cannot be taught*!

The true genius of any effective World Language teacher is found in her/his ability to create 'problematized' scenarios in the classroom that require language-based solutions.

The teacher as editor focused classroom relies on imitation as a foundational principle for instruction. In other words, the teacher serves as the conduit for all language. The teacher generates language; the students repeat after it. The teacher models sounds; the students imitate the sounds. The teacher presents the vocabulary; the students memorize it. The teacher explains grammar; the students transcribe it.

All well and good, except for one pressing consideration. *What if language is not primarily imitation?* Where does that leave the 'mastery' paradigm? This will be addressed during our discussion of the 'Proficiency' paradigm. Please stay tuned…

The two primary student outcomes produced by the mastery paradigm are metalanguage and identification. As such, students *know about* language (metalanguage) and are able to *identify* parts of speech with some degree of aplomb. They can spot a pluperfect subjunctive at 400 yards, and tell you why it is being used. Yet, generally they are unable to ask for the WC even if their bladders were about to implode. I might add, these students are limited in number as well, generally found among the 1-2% of those remaining in our ranks, as depicted in Figure 1.

Chapter 5

Reflections on Proficiency

In comparison to mastery, **Proficiency**, as an outcome, is quite different and seeks results that are equally as divergent. But to encourage Proficiency, we first need to define it. Why? Because unless we know what linguistic proficiency is, ***how will we recognize it when we see it?*** And if we can't recognize it, ***how can we assess it?***

After interviewing a myriad of teachers over the years regarding their operational definition of Proficiency, my respectful observation is that most language teachers really don't have one. And those that do, tend to have rambling notions filled largely with vagaries. I humbly offer you my operational definition of Proficiency immediately below. (Please memorize this, as there will be a test on this immediately following this section.)

Proficiency is the ability to produce and receive language that is *situationally appropriate...*

Note that I am offering an 'operational' definition. By that, I mean a definition that is so clear and compelling that it guides the way that one operates in the classroom. Figure 2 above illustrates that the primary focus of Proficiency is the acquisition of vocabulary. Why? Because vocabulary is, of nature, the readily communicative side of language. Lexical items come laced with meaning. That is not to imply that the Proficiency-oriented teacher completely expunges the study of grammar from the second language classroom. Rather she/he redefines the role of grammar, syntax and accuracy in the second language and allows the new definition to determine the amount of time on task. I will redefine that role for you shortly.

I am unable to overstate the importance of vocabulary as it relates to language and literacy. Worldwide, a child's first attempts at language are always rooted in lexicon. The first coherent utterance is almost always an attempt at a noun. A fractional percentage of the time, it is an exclamation, like 'NO!' (Some of us are 'blessed' with such offspring…) But never, EVER, in the recorded history of humanity, has the first utterance been structural. Kids just don't stand up in the crib and say 'brings'…

In the novice level language classroom, our students toil to construct sentences that are, in essence, almost completely comprised of lexical items. "Yo comer hamburguesas en la playa." (I eat hamburgers at the beach.) Although one might frown upon the unconjugated infinitive, it is important to recognize that an infinitive really is not structural, but rather lexical, until it is conjugated. That is why infinitives are found in the dictionary to start with. So, the example above really might best be viewed as a student's attempt to create language exclusively through lexical items, which is natural and indicative of all novice language acquirers. This would be the point of view of the Applied Linguist. The editor, conversely, would standardly end up in a rant about the number of times he/she has reminded the student that 'when it's YO, it's O!'

Furthermore, I adhere to the following 'organizing principles' pertaining to vocabulary:

- Vocabulary is a discrete subsystem of language that allows us to identify.
- We acquire vocabulary within the crucible of situation and problem- solving.
- We acquire vocabulary as we need it.
- We acquire vocabulary in context.
- We acquire vocabulary when we encounter more language than we own.
- We acquire vocabulary as we negotiate meaning.
- Vocabulary acquisition is an ongoing process.
- Vocabulary acquisition is a destination, not a point of departure.

The preceding 8 bulleted statements might best be distilled into one simple linguistic 'organizing principle': *Vocabulary is self-selected*. For this reason, the Proficiency-oriented classroom is student-centered and focused on language acquisition, unlike the mastery-driven classroom which is teacher-centered and focused on language teaching/learning.

The former encourages teacher as applied linguist, steadfastly in search for how the human mind creates and acquires language. The latter encourages teacher as editor.

Lest I be viewed as being opposed to grammar instruction, I would simply state that language teachers do not have the prerogative to ignore the grammar and syntax of the language that they advocate. The reason is both obvious and profound. There are no languages on the face of the earth that are without a grammar and syntax. Not even Esperanto, which is a contrived language that represents no specific culture.

Steven Pinker, in his book The Language Instinct, relates the following story. My paraphrase underscores the organic nature of structure and syntax in the language acquisition process.

> *After the Sandinistas established political control in Nicaragua, they gathered up all the deaf and mute children that they could find and placed them in camps. The purpose of the camps was not to educate, but rather to train the children to perform low level civil service tasks for the state. Within weeks, these children, heretofore 'incommunicado', began to sign to one another. The signing was crude, more 'gesticular circumlocution' than anything, filled with ample potential for 'miscommunication'. Nonetheless, the children created a 'pidgin' sign language from nothing. Eventually, a second group of children, equally as incommunicado as the first group, was commingled with the users of the newly minted pidgin sign language. Sensing that the pidgin was a good thing, the new group set about the task of 'creolizing' it; that is, overlaying an initial syntax and structure that minimized the potential for miscommunication. Today, this 'homegrown' sign language is the national sign language of Nicaragua.*

The lesson here is simple: Structure (grammar) and syntax are natural consequences of language acquisition, *not the cause*. Given the chance, they both will bubble up and take hold, even without direct instruction. Moreover, *the purpose of structure and syntax is not to initially create communication, but rather to reduce the potential for miscommunication.*

In order to illustrate this point, please consider Figure 3 below:

Figure 3

Imagine that you are driving home after school and the largest Mercedes Benz ever built flies by you as if you were standing still. Figure 3 represents the vanity plate on the back of this autobahn cruiser. What is the driver trying to communicate to you?...

Well... Given the fact that you are driving a 1993 Corolla, you might feel he is implying that he is 'better' than you. But then again, perhaps not... Maybe he's getting divorced and guess who is acquiring the Mercedes!... Maybe he's just plain 'bitter'... Still, he might not be that at all. Maybe he's just a lucky guy and his life has been like 'butter' and the Benz is just one small part of it!... Or is he just a famous homerun-hitting 'batter'?

There is no doubt that this vanity plate has created communication. It is improbable, however, that the author intended that there be four interpretations of his message. Maybe he's not bitter at all! Maybe he is a butter salesperson! Clearly, there is plenty of room for *miscommunication* here...

Now imagine we insert the letter 'I' between the 'B' and the first 'T' of the vanity plate above. What is the driver trying to communicate to us now?... Definitely 'bitter'... The addition of the letter 'I' has reduced the chance for miscommunication by 75%. In essence, this is the role of grammar and syntax in the language acquisition process. It is not to create communication... That is the role of vocabulary. The role of grammar is in the avoidance of miscommunication.

For those of you that are more logical-mathematical in mindset, here is an equation to ponder:

In this case, consonants are to vocabulary what vowels are to grammar and syntax. This is why vanity plates are largely comprised of consonants with vowels used to a far lesser degree.

Furthermore, when the word 'brings' is uttered out of context, what does it mean to you? How about 'rapidly'? You might be tempted to identify 'brings' as the 3rd person singular of the present tense of the indicative mood of the infinitive *to bring*. Or to classify 'rapidly' as an adverb, because it ends in *'ly'*, and further state that adverbs modify verbs, adjectives and other adverbs. It should be noted that this is not communication, but rather 'identification'.

As a result, the language teacher must create an instructional formula that recognizes both the primordial nature of vocabulary (and the time that it takes to develop it) and the inevitable emergence of grammar and syntax. This is a matter of recalibrating our usage of time in the World Language classroom based on the *nature of language*, not our own personal constructs of what that nature SHOULD be nor where we have to be in our textbooks by June.

Consider both, however, against the backdrop of just about any other noun... Say, 'apple', for instance. I'm sure that there might be someone out there whose mind might drift to identifying 'apple' as a noun. If so, you have just exposed yourself as being mastery-driven. However, I would conjecture that you, the reader, conjured up an image of 'apple-ness' instead... A fruit, red, round, crunchy, pie, motherhood, New York City, William Tell, your dentist, computers, Original Sin! Vocabulary comes laced with meaning. Structure does not. In fact, the only structural point that we teach that is readily communicative is commands. Do you sense the difference in communicative value between 'Bring' and 'Brings'? In the former, you probably feel a sense of somehow being engaged in the process of 'bringing' something to someone somewhere. 'Brings' offers no personal engagement whatsoever. In other words, it doesn't 'resonate' with you. In other words, it doesn't communicate. Besides that, if you go around giving commands all day, no one will want to communicate with you anyway!

The single most common gesture used by pre-linguistic children is pointing with the index finger. Why would a child make such a gesture? To find out whether a word is an adjective or an adverb? Hardly! It is a request for identification of objects in a world that, for the child at this point, has no labels. Lexical items help us to make sense of the world around us. The starting point for human language is lexical in nature, not structural. This should offer us clear guidance as to what we should be emphasizing in our classrooms from day one as we initiate our students into the world of L2.

My purpose for begging your indulgence on this point is uniquely to float this idea... *That perhaps the reason why the vast majority of our students do not end up communicating in a second language to any substantive degree is because our classrooms are primarily focused upon those aspects of language that are largely non-communicative.* Furthermore, I contend that the primary reason most students flee our ranks is due to hyper focus on those structural matters.

The issue for us, as Applied Linguists, is not whether we teach grammar and syntax. To the contrary! They are natural components to and consequences of all languages. Left to its own devices, any language will evolve its own grammar and syntax over time. The real issue at hand is understanding why they need to be taught and clearly 'defining' the role of grammar and syntax in the language acquisition process; taming the beast, if you would.

Before concerning ourselves with miscommunication, what must first exist? Communication, of course. And that very communication will always be less than accurate. Simply stated, *grammatical accuracy is a destination, not a point of departure.*

Unlike the mastery-driven classroom, the Proficiency-orientated classroom is student-centered and acquisition-focused largely due to the fact that language is 100% an acquired ability.

There is good reason to believe that no one ever has actually been *taught* a language; that we are all 100% responsible for the language that we own. (*Many of you who have been considering a move to real estate sales probably feel that I have just provided you the perfect reason to jump ship!*) Not so! This fact challenges the language *teacher* to desist from serving as the conduit for all language activity and to find ways to encourage kids to <u>select it</u>...

Neither you nor I own one word in any language that we did not *personally select,* drawn from the crucible of situation and problem-solving. Selection of vocabulary requires opportunity to do so, and plenty of it. The following personal anecdote should clearly illustrate the concept of linguistic self-selection. (See Figure 2)

> *I was seated at a corner table in an Italian restaurant in New Jersey, away from windows, with my back to the wall; a custom born of viewing The Godfather Trilogy too many times.*
>
> *At the neighboring table, seven adults and one three year old boy were seated. I use 'seated' as a relative term with reference to the three year old as little boys of that age rarely do what we refer to as 'sitting'. More precisely, he was twitching, sliding, swinging and generally trying to find as many uses for his bolster seat as possible during the meal. I lost track at use number 17... By the time the adults had ordered their respective meals, I had already finished my antipasto and was now contentedly awaiting my main course. Everyone at the neighboring table had ordered substantial meals, with the exception of the little boy, who was to dine upon the obligatory burger, accompanied by fries, soda and a scoop of vanilla ice cream. Watching this child was like watching Mount St. Helen. The question at hand was not whether there would be an eruption, but rather when that eruption might occur. After two bites of his burger, a few nibbles of his fries, downing the entire soda and devouring the ice cream, he was now done! Unfortunately, his adult dinner mates were just beginning. He was not pleased by the prospects of having to endure this much longer.*

At precisely the hour and fifteen minute mark, the eruption occurred. Unable to control himself any longer, the three year old threw his hands up in the air, brought them back down on his chubby little knees and, in a surprisingly loud voice, intoned the following phrase: "Let's get the h_ _l outta' here!" The restaurant, which heretofore had been filled with quiet conversation and the sound of tinkling china and silverware, now fell to a hush. All eyes turned to the child, who now oozed down into his bolster seat in an attempt to attain safe harbor somewhere below the table surface. I, of course, did all I could not to laugh out loud! Still, the best part of this entire interlude centered upon the look that the mother shot across the table to the father. If a glare could vaporize human tissue, this man would have been become particles in the atmosphere. Her message, attested to by the kinesics of her body language, went something like this: "You see! Don't I tell you not to talk that way in front of the baby! You see how he ***IMITATES*** *you!"*

To say that the 3 year old simply imitated his father would be to imply that the child was a hapless victim of ambient or 'drive-by' language; that the child was the 'passive' recipient of language that he never intended to own. To the contrary, I would submit to you that humans aggressively select language that is pertinent to their lives; language that helps them to resolve problems; language that is useful and colorful. We select our own lexicon.

Did the father use the phrase that the child so skillfully deployed? Beyond a doubt! Was the child present when the father used the phrase? Clearly! But, the 3 year old heard it and said to himself, "I like that! I'll file that for future reference!" And so he did. And the fact that he waited one hour and fifteen minutes to deploy proves to me that this was not an act of imitation. Just as his father, he waited to deploy until the situation was intolerable.

The statement was age inappropriate, but devastatingly 'proficient'…

Language teachers are singularly patient people; patient with those around them who haven't a clue as to the role of second language acquisition in the American curriculum; patient dealing with popular mythologies declaring multilingualism as somehow outside the scope of the American mind; patient with their students.

On any given school day, language teachers are treated to renditions of the language they teach that are reminiscent of the language of instruction, but still quite a bit removed. This requires an inordinate amount of patience as well as a robust sense of humor.

> *"J'ai avoir un beaucoup a amusant a tu classe! J'adore French parce que a tu! J'espère tu es moi professeur ensuite un an..."*

> *"Hola, señor. Yo ser Ricardo. Yo visitar Mexico despues mi primero el año de escola secondario y yo gustar muy. Ahora, yo trabajar con el amigo de Mexico también. El ayudar me muy a la lugar de trabajo. Gracias por usted tiempo. Yo necesitar comer ahora..."*

There are those that would quickly assign the two preceding performances to the realm of 'Franglais' or 'Spanglish'; that is, hopelessly substandard mixtures of the native language (L1) and the target language (L2); mixtures that will fossilize and inevitably doom both the student, as well as all of humanity, to failure.

First and foremost, I would contend that these performances are not examples of 'Franglais' or 'Spanglish'. To earn that moniker, the errors would have to be intentional. What we normally hear from our students on any given day is their best attempt to approximate the language of instruction. The 'errors' that accompany these performances are not intentional per se, but rather intuitive guesses offered up by the students. Moreover, we as language teachers must learn to welcome these errors because they are, in fact, our reality. *The alternative is silence or the regurgitation of memorized material... The incessant drone of the chromatic scale.*

Dr. Larry Selinker, Professor Emeritus, New York University, provides us with a name for such performances... Interlanguage. (See Figure 2) He reminds us that this is a critical stage in the language acquisition process, serving as the link between L1 and L2. Furthermore, he posits the notion that when Interlanguage is expunged from the classroom, the language acquisition process is subverted. I would contend that this is precisely why so many students exposed to the mastery approach end up essentially non-functional in the L2.

The single most common strategy deployed by language acquirers at any age is to move aspects of their L1 into L2, thus creating an L3, or, if you would, Interlanguage. Despite the World Language teacher's best attempts to keep the L1 and L2 separate, the eventuality of commingling is inevitable. Figures 4, 5 and 7 will graphically chart the process:

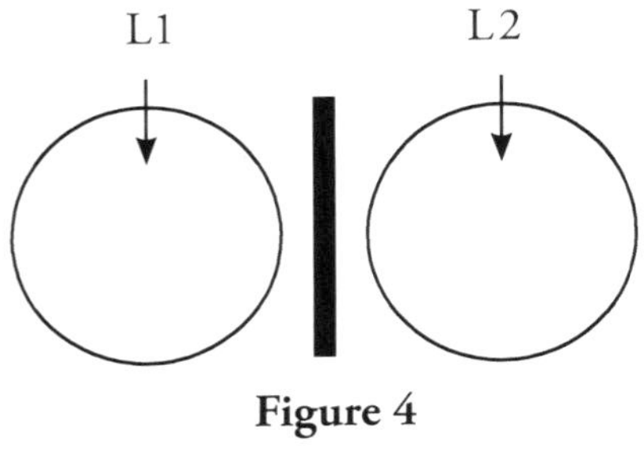

Figure 4

Figure 4 illustrates the initial instructional dynamic set up in the World Language classroom. The circle to the left represents the L1 of the student. To facilitate, let's say it is English, *(or the language formerly known as English.)* The circle to the right is the target language or L2. Concerns over 'linguistic interference' often lead teachers to employ strategies designed to keep L1 and L2 separate or 'target language only' strategies; thus, the line drawn between the 2 circles. However, the arrow in figure 5 implies that, of nature, language learners move L1 into L2 in an attempt to function in and understand the L2.

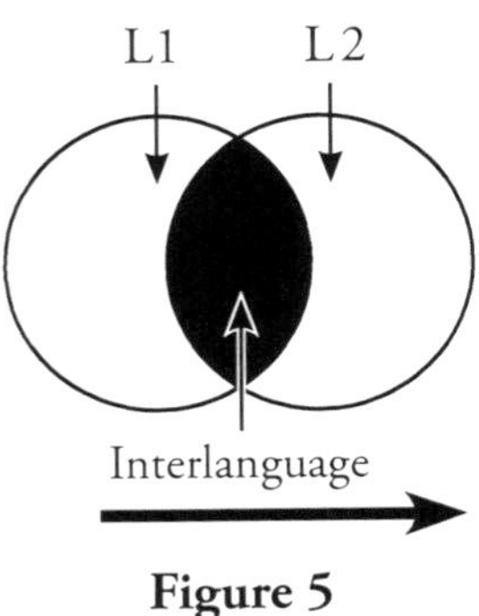

Figure 5

When L1 merges with L2, a third language is generated (darkened area). It is neither English nor the target language, but rather a hybrid or 'pidgin' language. As we have never had adequate terminology to describe this phenomenon, it has commonly been referred to as 'Spanglish', 'Franglais', 'Chinglish', 'broken English', etc. Interlanguage, however, must be viewed differently. It opens up opportunities for students to risk-take, to be vulnerable and to use their intuition. It provides students with a chance to actually 'own' the L2 at some level, even though their performances contain numerous errors.

And plentiful the errors will be. But, it is important to note that an 'error' is not at all the same as a 'mistake'. Figure 6 below will illustrate the distinctions.

Error	**Mistake**
• Inventive	• Fossilized
• Dynamic	• Static
• Transitional	• Permanent
• Intuitive	• Conscious

Figure 6

Error is a byproduct of the inventive process. As the student grapples to create the L2, he/she invents language on the spot. Just as when the aspiring musician attempts to play jazz, missed notes must be anticipated. Though the delivery is less than perfect, it is still infinitely more engaging than listening to the chromatic scale played incessantly.

Mistakes, on the other hand, are reflective of fossilized, engrained and repetitive language patterns. Over a period of time, linguistic mistakes become the natural and comfortable choice for usage. Unlike errors, mistakes are not caused by early encounters with a language. They are the byproduct of long term patterning.

Error is dynamic. As such, it might best be described as 'non-standard language on its way to becoming standard.' The Interlanguage that our students produce, should it be permitted, will evolve and change, always moving toward standardization.

Mistakes are static in that they are embedded in and accepted as part of the permanent repertoire of the language user. They are not destined to evolve or change and their remediation requires a focused effort on his or her part.

Because error is dynamic, of nature it is transitional. The Proficiency-oriented teacher understands this phenomenon and is not concerned to any great degree about fossilization. Error serves as part of the superstructure of the bridge that leads from monolingualism to multilingualism.

Mistakes are permanent, embedded linguistic behaviors that are reversed only with considerable Language Arts remediation. As such, they are more likely to be exhibited by native speakers than L2 language acquirers.

Error is born of intuitive selection. It is the byproduct of the lexicon, structure and syntax of the L1 being applied to aspects of the L2. Language acquirers literally 'guess' at how something might be said or written in the L2 based on their limited exposure to that L2 and the patterns of their native tongue. The errors that arise are largely unintentional.

Mistakes are born of conscious selection. Quite often the individual knows better, but elects to overlook the standard form. It is important to note that *language identifies you as a member of a group*. And frequently, acceptance and group recognition outweigh the imperative for accurate language usage. Mistakes are largely intentional in nature. Once again, they are more likely to be exhibited by native speakers than L2 language acquirers.

My advice? Know the difference between errors and mistakes. It will improve your classroom results enormously!

There are essentially 2 basic types of errors that we should anticipate from our students from day to day and year to year: Interlinguistic Errors and Intralinguistic Errors.

Interlinguistic errors are brought about by the clash of two disparate linguistic systems. For example, the use of object pronouns in English might best be transcribed in the following syntactical/grammatical formula:

Subject + Verb + Object Pronoun/ I + see + it

In French and Spanish, however, the syntactical/grammatical formula is different from their English counterpart:

Subject + Object Pronoun + Verb/ Je + le + vois/ (Yo) + lo + veo/ I + it + see

For the native English speaker attempting to acquire French or Spanish, the internal software program, installed at an early age, supports **Subject + Verb + Object Pronoun.** It takes a considerable amount of time for the new French or Spanish software to boot up supporting **Subject + Object Pronoun + Verb.** In the interim, there is dissonance, or interlinguistic errors; to wit: **Je vois le/ (Yo) veo lo.** (I see it.)

Recognizing interlinguistic errors for what they are and anticipating them from year to year will serve to support a Proficiency-orientated classroom as well as to maintain teacher sanity. It is the 'modus operandi' of the applied linguist and anathema to the editor.

Intralinguistic errors are brought about by the unique peculiarities of a given L2 to which there are no comparisons in L1; for example, gender of nouns. It is common among Romance languages to require that nouns be assigned either a masculine or feminine gender that dictates the usage of the respective definite or indefinite article. As a result, a student might ask why the Spanish word 'silla' (chair) is feminine. The teacher might respond that this is the case because the word ends in 'a'. This, of course, is a completely inadequate answer as the student is looking to relate this information to something similar in English. As a result, errors are made recurrently.

Another example might be the usage of the verbs 'ser' and 'estar' in Spanish, both meaning 'to be', but nevertheless deployed under different circumstances. In English, there is but one verb 'to be' and it is used universally. Whereas the native English speaker might take years to develop a feel for the appropriate usage of these two verbs in Spanish, any two-year-old Hispanic child can manipulate them with complete ease and facility. The English speaker finds no comparative in English and thus must acquire the proper usage the hard way; by making tons of errors.

Just as with Interlinguistic errors, Intralinguistic errors are a natural part of the language acquisition process and should be anticipated, if not celebrated.

As represented by the darkened area in Figure 7 that follows, Interlanguage, if permitted, will increase exponentially in the classroom as students continue to risk-take, to be vulnerable and to use intuition. This can produce unsettling emotions in the World Language teacher as he/she ponders the reaction of next year's teacher to this less than standard language. In other words, there are concerns regarding 'fossilization'.

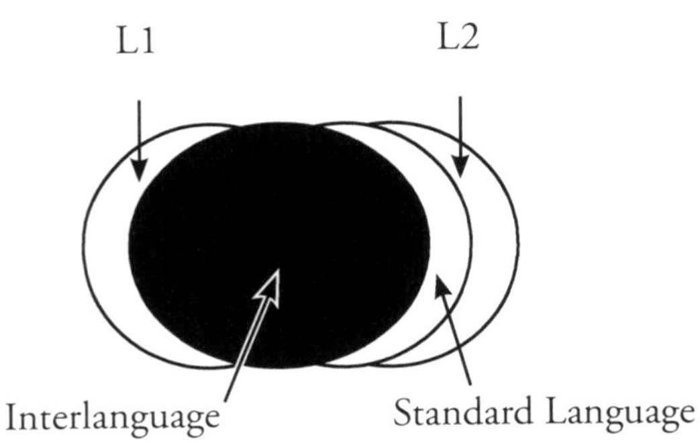

Figure 7

Linguistic fossilization occurs when an individual's language no longer continues to evolve, expand or move toward more standard usage. It is suspended at a certain level. Many language teachers fear this as a consequence of permitting Interlanguage in the classroom. If they allow less than standard language, those patterns will embed permanently. I would like to argue to the contrary. For fossilization to occur in L2 acquirers, two conditions must exist:

1. The acquirer must have enough L2 to fossilize.

2. Through behavior, the acquirer demonstrates a desire to fossilize the L2.

In response to the first condition, I would simply state that most beginning and even intermediate World Language students do not own enough language to begin the fossilization process. And even if they did, why would they want to if they were already functioning at some level and meeting with success?

Regarding the second condition, I believe that individuals consciously choose to suspend the growth of their language. They don't travel. They avoid opportunities to use their L2. They don't read and view in L2. As such, it is often the native speaker that fossilizes her/his language, not the L2 acquirer. This is one reason why the LI of so many families that emigrate to the United States disappears by second generation.

This can also be the case with cultural awareness. On a trip to Italy, I found myself conversing in Italian with a resident of the Tuscany region. This gentleman made the statement that people of Italian heritage in the United States are often more *'Italian'* than Italian nationals. Curious about his statement, I asked for clarification. The conversation, translated into English, went something like this:

Italian Gentleman: Italian Americans are more Italian than we are…

John: I don't understand what you mean.

Italian Gentleman: Well… How old was your grandmother when she traveled to the United States?

John: She was 8.

Italian Gentleman: Did she return to Italy from time to time?

John: No. Never, sadly.

Italian Gentleman: And growing up at home with her… Did you celebrate the saints' days?

John: Yes… Are you kiddin' me?!

Italian Gentleman: And did your grandmother make the fried dough and sprinkle confectioner's sugar on top to celebrate?

John: You bet! They were delicious!. I loved them as a kid!

Italian Gentleman: Well... We don't do that anymore.

Cultural awareness, just as language, can fossilize when left unattended. But normally it is a byproduct of a conscious decision on the individual's part.

It is time for our profession to shake its fear of 'fossilization' as it relates to the L2 classroom. Mythologies regarding fossilization in the language classroom support mastery instruction as defined in Chapter 4 and impede, if not entirely expunge, the critical element of Interlanguage from the L2 acquisition scenario. By embracing the notion of Interlanguage, we have everything to gain and so very little to lose. It is time to move onward and upward!

It would be legitimate at this juncture for a language teacher to question when, if and how students ever move toward a more standard usage of the L2. The explanation begins with a somewhat rhetorical question: *If you were an apartment dweller, how much money would you spend renovating that apartment?* Logic would dictate the response. *Not much, if anything!* And why not? The answer would be direct and uncomplicated. *Because I don't own it!* Thus, the axiom that comes forth from all of this is quite clear ...

People DO NOT renovate what they do not own!

Let's apply that very same axiom to the language acquisition process. Interlanguage (the darkened area in figures 5 and 7) is a student's first attempt at ownership of linguistic property. And just like the first real estate that we might purchase, the initial structure might not be everything that we ever dreamed of. Instead, it might rightly be something quite humble; a handyman's special; a fixer-upper! But, it is ours! And there is 'pride in ownership'! So, we begin to renovate; perhaps first by buying a few gallons of paint and painting the walls and, if there is some money left over, by carpeting the bedroom...

Thus it is with language acquisition. The small corona that is found just to the right of the darkened area in Figure 7 illustrates the fact that gradual standardization is the byproduct of Interlanguage.

The mastery approach to language teaching illogically insists that the student renovate prior to ownership; that she/he study the grammar of a given language before the language is personally owned at some level; that 'renovation' precede 'ownership'.

Again, it is important to remember that linguistic accuracy is a byproduct of acquisition, and not the inverse.

In the end result, this question falls to each of us as World Language teachers:

Just what type of linguistic mortgage broker am I? Will I float the kids a loan so that they can own some 'linguistic real estate', no matter how humble? Or will I keep them in linguistic tenements , never knowing the joy of ownership?

Chapter 6

The Cognitive Benefits of Bilingualism/Biliteracy

Prior to 1960, it was believed that the nature of the brain and its functions were fixed and were strictly a byproduct of genetics. The watershed research of Dr. Marion Diamond, Professor of Anatomy at the University of California Berkeley, challenged this thinking in 1964 when she introduced her theory of 'brain plasticity'. This theory stated that anything done to enrich the human brain, *at any age*, enriches the cerebral cortex, thus increasing learning capacity. Furthermore, she outlined 5 broad areas in the human experience that are essential to developing a better brain: diet, exercise, challenge, newness and love. Conversely, anything that impoverishes the human brain diminishes learning capacity.

The third of Diamond's areas, *challenge*, will serve as the focus of this chapter.

Since the early 1960s, an ever growing body of research has come forth indicating that bilingualism can be of great personal advantage. Prior to that time, however, the general consensus among researchers was quite the contrary, posturing bilingualism as a handicap that atrophied linguistic and cognitive development in children. In comparison to their monolingual counterparts, the prediction was that bilingual children would inevitably have smaller overall vocabularies, would never achieve full competency in either language and would generally exhibit reduced cognitive abilities. Although it is now widely accepted that bilingual children tend to own smaller overall vocabularies *initially*, this distinction generally remediates by age 5, with bilingual children demonstrating more robust vocabularies than their monolingual counterparts.

Maria Polinsky, Professor of Linguistics at Harvard University, notes that the preeminence of monolingualism over the years has been significantly underwritten by the economic reach and geographical mass of countries such as China (Mandarin), Russia (Russian) and the United States (English), with bilingualism viewed as the exception and not the rule. Yet, according to Professor Polinsky, it is actually monolingualism that is the "aberration", with the majority of the other smaller world states being bilingual. (Please see Figure 8.) Statistically, in fact, 66% of the world's children are presently being raised bilingually.

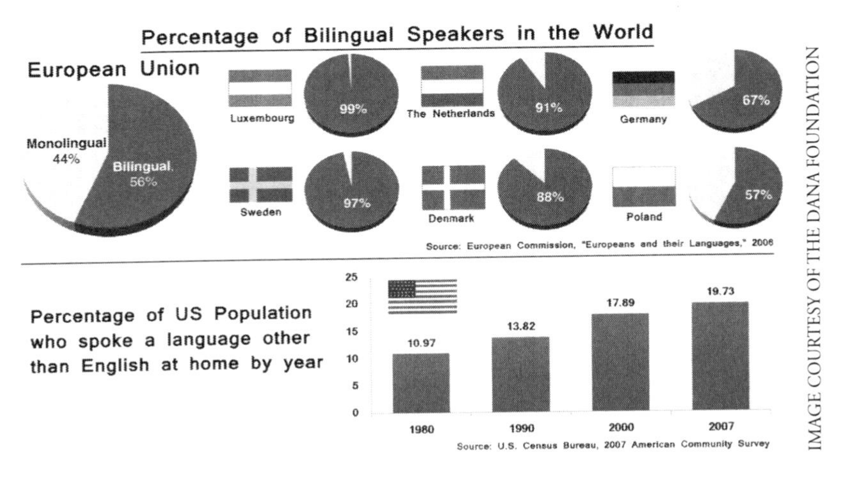

Figure 8

The largely flawed research models employed prior to the 1960s were also responsible for the emergent negative attitudes toward bilingualism. Influencing factors, such as socioeconomic status (SES), gender and age were largely disregarded as monolingual and bilingual study participants were compared as a group but not matched based on the aforementioned influencing factors. Once factors such as SES, gender and age were eventually systematically applied to the research studies, findings were virtually reversed, with bilinguals enjoying significant advantage over monolinguals, not only in verbal and non-verbal assessments, but in those that highlighted mental flexibility as well.

It is important to note that both languages are constantly operating within the bilingual brain. As a result, these languages are continually battling one another for preeminence, creating a 'challenge' for the human brain and causing what is referred to as 'linguistic interference'. The consequences are particularly apparent when one of the two languages owned is clearly dominant over the other. Delivering or comprehending a message in L2 can be a daunting task if L1 is always interfering. This creates a need, in the bilingual brain, to control (inhibit) the amount and variety of language accessed in any given circumstance. In order to hit a balance, the bilingual brain counts on what is referred to as its 'executive functions'.

The executive functions are a set of cognitive regulatory processes housed primarily, but not exclusively, in the prefrontal cortex of the brain. These processes help to select, monitor and control human behavior based on situations and personally selected goals. Among those processes are problem solving, mental flexibility, attention control, inhibitory control and the ability to task switch on the fly.

It is important to note that executive functions develop gradually over the entire human lifespan and can be affected negatively, as well, due to any confluence of events such as neurological and/or psychiatric disorders.

In order to more fully understand executive functions, definition of the various processes might be in order:

- Problem Solving: The ability to resolve issues by employing more complex thinking.
- Mental Flexibility: The ability to adapt cognitively to circumstances.
- Attention Control: The ability to focus intently on critical factors.
- Inhibitory Control: The ability to initially disregard factors that are not of immediate importance.
- Task Switching: The ability to spontaneously and simultaneously manage tasks and situations.

Moreover, each time a bilingual speaks (output) or listens (input), these processes are automatically stimulated and triggered, causing mental challenge, thus rendering the respective areas of the brain more robust. As a result, the research notes that bilinguals are generally more adept at tasks that require conflict resolution (problem solving). What one does with the brain, impacts the brain both in its function and in its composition.

Bilinguals also appear to be more adept than their monolingual counterparts at switching tasks. This skill is largely derived from the constant need for bilinguals to ignore competing perceptual information (inhibitory control) in favor of the more relevant details dictated by the situation or context (attention control). Furthermore, bilinguals appear to move from task to task more rapidly (mental flexibility), signifying better cognitive control in general. Needless to say, these characteristics exert an overwhelmingly positive influence on academic learning, learning in general and employment opportunity in the United States as well as around the world.

It is important to note that the cognitive benefits of bilingualism may be enjoyed throughout life, not only for those raised bilingually, but even for those attempting to acquire a second language later in life. Those benefits include enriched cognitive control, neural enhancement, increased social interaction across cultures and improved metalinguistic awareness (manipulating language systems). It is precisely this improvement in metalinguistic awareness that enhances understanding of language systems and fosters better comprehension of what is heard, read and viewed. In other words, we find that literacy is a direct outcome of enriched language and not the contrary.

Bilinguals generally outperform their monolingual counterparts, not only in spoken language, but in assessments of reading ability as well.

A preponderance of the research, both past and present, still tends to focus upon the impact of bilingualism in early childhood. Nevertheless, there is growing interest regarding the effects that bilingualism has upon the aging process. As humans beings age, there is a gradual and natural decline in cognitive prowess. In its most extreme state, this decline can manifest itself in the form of dementia or Alzheimer's Disease, with the individual eventually losing all perception of self; the *cognitive reserve* being virtually depleted. As stated by Dr. Marion Diamond, "Take away the brain, you take away the person."

The term 'cognitive reserve' pertains to the sum total of cognitive processes and executive functions each individual maintains within the brain. As it relates to human existence, it is clearly imperative to maintain that reserve for as long as possible, thus forestalling the onset of general cognitive decline. Although bilingualism will not serve as a permanent hedge against dementia or Alzheimer's Disease, research shows that, on balance, bilinguals who fall victim to such cognitive disorders experience their first symptoms 5.1 years later than their monolingual counterparts and are diagnosed 4.3 years later. (Please see Figure 9.) It is believed that this is the direct result of the executive functions being recurrently challenged and deployed as they work to control and manipulate two languages existing side by side in the bilingual brain. Thus, bilingualism has the capacity to modify the neural structure and activity of the aging brain, resulting in improved memory, more mental sharpness and rerouting of neural paths potentially damaged by the aging process.

First Symptoms Monolingual **75** Years	**First Symptoms** Bilingual **80.1** Years
Diagnosis Monolingual **75** Years	**Diagnosis** Bilingual **79.3** Years

Figure 9

In summary, growing contemporary research recognizes the significant cognitive benefits that bilingualism brings to the human experience. We are now aware that the human brain is not predestined from birth, but rather adapts to circumstances throughout life. It can be enriched or impoverished at any time, thus expanding or limiting the capacity to learn.

It is now apparent that being bilingual challenges and, in effect, exercises the brain, developing it in ways never before imagined, modifying its function and its very composition. The rewards are many and varied. Among them, we can count enhanced ability to problem solve, greater mental flexibility, improved focus and attention control, heightened ability to multitask, task switch and think in more complicated ways along with enhanced reading comprehension, semantic processing of words and employment opportunity. Furthermore, bilingualism appears to postpone the deleterious impact of cognitive disorders and cognitive decline. As researchers Ellen Bialystok and Kenji Hakuta remind us in their book In Other Words, being bilingual brings much more to humanity than just functionality in two languages and appreciation for other cultures. There are vast cognitive benefits to be enjoyed and celebrated as well. This fact may be best summed up in their own words…

"The knowledge of two languages is greater than the sum of its parts."

Chapter 7

Six Best Practices for the Language Classroom

Language is a common phenomena that comes freely to virtually everyone with the exception of those that may suffer overwhelming physical and/or cognitive handicaps. Yet, the emergence of language is still largely the subject of debate; a debate that has ensued for centuries. In fact, for discussion purposes, it may be best to view language acquisition as *a mystery, shrouded in a puzzle, wrapped within an enigma.* Nonetheless, an ever growing research base has accrued over time leading us closer and closer to an understanding of how the human mind creates and acquires language.

There have been several methods that have made their appearance in US schools, with most eventually waning. A brief sampling of certain historical trends, leading to current practices, might be in order at this point so as to grasp our evolution as linguists. As a point of clarification, it should be noted that the terms 'approach' and 'method' are not considered interchangeable herewithin. An approach might best be defined as the sum total of beliefs (organizing principles) that one holds regarding language acquisition. A method refers to the techniques that one deploys to realize those beliefs.

Prior to the introduction of modern languages into the American curriculum in the 19th century, Latin and classical Greek were the only languages offered. Their study was thought to develop mental discipline along with a more refined and educated citizenry. The instructional focus centered on grammatical knowledge, discrete word study, reading of ancient literary and historical texts and translation of said texts into English.

It was only natural that initial modern language study should follow the same pattern of instruction and led to what has since been referred to as the Grammar-Translation Method. This method prevailed in the 19th century classroom and continued well into the 20th.

- **Grammar-Translation Method**: Students learn grammatical rules and translate sentences from Latin/Greek into the native language (L1). The method has two main goals: to enable students to read and translate Latin/Greek literature and to further students' general intellectual development.

In reaction to the Grammar-Translation Method, the beginning of the 20th century heralded the arrival of Direct Method.

- **Direct Method**: With the stated goal of students learning how to communicate in another language, Direct Method is characterized by instruction conducted solely in the target language, grammar taught indirectly, the absence of translation, with the primary focus on vocabulary acquisition and oral language. Known also as the 'Natural Method', Direct Method supports the notion that a student should acquire a second language in much the same manner as she/he acquires the native tongue.

Behavioral Psychologists, such as B. F. Skinner, believed that all human behavior, including language, is a result of repetition and reinforcement. Thus, the middle decades of the 20th century saw the inception of the Audio-lingual Method.

- **Audio-lingual Method**: Although a four skills approach, the Audio-lingual Method focuses primarily on listening and speaking with reading and writing deemphasized. Rote memorization of dialogues act as the centerpiece of the method along with repetitious pattern drills designed to inculcate certain linguistic patterns in students. The 'language laboratory' made its first debut as an important instructional aid. Much like Direct Method, the usage of L1 is discouraged, but to a lesser degree.

A seismic shift in thinking occurred in the latter part of the 20th century and continues to the present. With the arrival of Second Language Acquisition (SLA) theory, priorities have shifted from methodology to Applied Linguistics; from language teaching/ learning to language acquisition.

- **Second Language Acquisition (SLA) Theory**: Stephen Krashen, Professor Emeritus at the University of Southern California, is a major proponent of SLA. It is through the various hypotheses set forth by Dr. Krashen that we begin to understand the 'nature' of language and the fact that any instructional methodology employed must respect that nature for it to be effective. That is not to say that method is unimportant. It simply reorders instructional priorities. It serves as a reminder that 'best practices' are to be considered commensurate to their impact upon eventual functionality. Four of Dr. Krashen's major hypotheses are listed below:
    - Acquisition-learning Hypothesis: The fact that languages are 'acquired' subconsciously as opposed to being 'learned' discretely. Individuals are generally unaware of the process as well as the aspects acquired. Language acquisition is largely a random process with knowledge stored subconsciously in the brain.
    - Input Hypothesis: The fact that all output of language is a byproduct of 'comprehensible input' (CI). The more CI is provided by the teacher, the more it is sought by the student.
    - Monitor Hypothesis: The fact that consciously learned language provides a monitor (editor) for previously acquired language. As a result, accuracy in a language is the eventual byproduct of language acquisition. Language acquisition is not the byproduct of accuracy. In support of that thinking, Freeman and Freeman remind us that "the conventions of language should not impede the invention of language."

- Affective Filter Hypothesis: The fact that anxiety blocks both input and output of language. Reducing that anxiety for the student both environmentally and personally enhances language acquisition.

It is against this backdrop of Second Language Acquisition theory that I highlight the following six 'best practices' that support language acquisition, and therefore enhance the opportunity for L2 functionality for both English Language Learners (ELL) and students studying Languages Other Than English (LOTE):

1. Use Comparative Linguistics: It serves no constructive instructional purpose to ignore the role that the first language (L1) plays in the acquisition of a second language (L2). In fact, doing so may completely undermine the acquisition of the second language. One of the primary functions of a language is to identify an individual as a member of a group. Devaluing a student's native language is, in effect, asking that individual to relinquish ties with his/her group and/or culture. It is equally important to note that when one is acquiring a second language, the tendency is to move L1 into L2, thus causing linguistic interference. Whenever possible, compare both languages for similarities, such as cognates. It is useful to contrast, as well, particularly as it relates to structure, syntax and situational usage.

2. Provide Comprehensible Input: When a student is in the midst of acquiring a second language, he/she moves from the concrete to the abstract. Therefore, visuals, gesture, music, dance, facial expressions, etc., all enhance language acquisition and should be incorporated as primary techniques in the L2 classroom. Everything done instructionally to assist students with input (listening, reading, and viewing), encourages output of language (speaking, writing). The more instruction 'provides' comprehensible input, the more students will 'seek' it.

3. Focus on Authentic Language Acquisition: Language is primarily a device deployed by humans to resolve problems. It emerges as a byproduct of context and situation. As such, the language classroom needs to reflect the 'purpose' and 'nature' of language. *Authentic* language acquisition classrooms encourage students to acquire language within real-world contexts, using the language to resolve real-world problems. In the traditional language classroom, the target language typically is not used for problem resolution. Rather, it is the very study of the target language that becomes the problem. Authentic language acquisition is student driven, interdisciplinary and connects the construction of new knowledge with a student's existing knowledge and experience. Among other characteristics, an authentic language acquisition classroom includes:

- inquiry
- exploration
- discourse
- collaboration
- reflection
- problem resolution
- diversity of outcomes

4. Use Authentic Assessment: Authentic acquisition of language demands *frequent* authentic assessment, both formative and summative. This form of assessment is performance-based, tends to focus on contextualized tasks, and seeks a demonstrable 'end product'; one that is rooted in the real world. Some broad categories include:

- Public demonstration of a given skill or modes of communication (interpersonal, presentational, interpretive).
- Role playing and simulations.
- Studio portfolios (art, musical composition, photography, poetry, essays, vocal and instrumental musical performance, etc.).

Authentic Assessment is the measurement of intellectual accomplishments that are worthwhile, significant, and meaningful.

In many cases, it is a product that is intended to be shared with an audience and, therefore, open to critique. Whereas traditional assessment follows the curriculum and seeks one correct answer, authentic assessment employs 'backwards design', with the curriculum based upon the assessment as well as inviting a diversity of possible outcomes.

5. Implement a 'Communication First' Environment: In order to encourage language production (speaking/writing), a 'linguistically friendly' classroom environment needs to be established; one where a student is free to acquire a second language without fear of ridicule; where one is rewarded for what one knows as opposed to being penalized for what one does not know as yet. There is an intimate relationship between language acquisition and an individual's willingness to take linguistic risks, to be vulnerable and to use intuition. Loosely defined, linguistic risk-taking is the willingness, on the part of the language student, to confront more language than what she/he owns. Vulnerability is the willingness, on a student's part, to err for the broader goal of communication. Intuition implies student willingness to skim and scan for information and to seek comprehensible input whenever possible. Moreover, a student can only exhibit these psycholinguistic characteristics to the extent that their teacher supports them instructionally. Belief in *communication first* can serve to encourage such a classroom environment. It is always tempting to focus initially on the language arts of a given language in an attempt to guarantee accurate L2 communication. Yet, as Dr. Krashen reminds us, accuracy is a byproduct of acquisition and not the inverse. Seeing accuracy as a destination rather than a point of departure enhances the opportunity for language acquisition.

6. Hold rigorous, yet realistic expectations: It is imperative to establish performance expectations for students that are both rigorous and realistic. Rigorous to the extent that course content provides challenge and realistic to the extent that varied student backgrounds are taken into account. As such, a more balanced

approach comprised of social language proficiency (informal register), academic language proficiency (formal register), grammar and literacy is preferable. Opportunity to read and discuss literary texts as well as informational texts can assist in this balancing process. Additionally, arranging students both homogeneously and heterogeneously in small groups, based on linguistic experience, can also be beneficial.

To summarize, our knowledge of how the human mind creates and acquires language has steadily increased over time. Latin and Classical Greek were the initial languages studied in the American school house. Language classrooms focused on the reading and writing of their respective literatures and histories. The popular method of instruction at that time featured grammatical analysis, vocabulary study, along with translation of original texts into English and was referred to as the Grammar-Translation Method. Despite the eventual appearance of modern language study in the American curriculum, the Grammar Translation-Method continued to be employed and its influence extended well into the 20th century.

The 20th century brought an awareness that 4 skills, not just 2, were inherent to the languages taught in the school house: listening, speaking, reading and writing. As a result, Direct Method made its appearance. This method, although 4 skills based, focused primarily on listening and speaking with the classroom conducted exclusively in the target language. Known also as the Natural Method, it was anticipated that students would acquire L2 much the same way they acquired L1.

The Audio-lingual Method made its debut in the mid to latter part of the 20th century. Heavily influenced by Behavioralist Psychology, it was believed that students could be 'patterned' into a second language. The memorization of situationalized dialogues and rote pattern drills were the hallmarks of the method. The language laboratory made its initial debut, as well.

Simply stated, the goal of the 21st century language classroom is *functionality*. Pursuant to the increasing influence of Second

Language Acquisition (SLA) theory, 'methodology', though still important, is secondary to 'approach'. Method is seen as the byproduct of organizing principles drawn from Applied Linguistics. As a result, the discussion of 'best practices' no longer centers *primarily* on specific techniques used to deliver a discrete instructional point; for example, understanding the difference between completed and repeated past actions and how that difference impacts past tense usage. Instead, best practices reflect a broad, research-based conceptual approach believed to encourage language acquisition.

Thus, functionality in a second language can be achieved by using Comparative Linguistics, providing comprehensible input (CI), targeting authentic language acquisition, using authentic assessment, implementing a 'communication first' environment and holding rigorous, yet realistic expectations.

Chapter 8

Vocabulary Acquisition and Music

In Chapter 5, the topic of vocabulary acquisition was raised. Let's revisit three of the premises posited:

- We acquire vocabulary within the crucible of situation and problem-solving.
- We acquire vocabulary as we need it.
- We acquire vocabulary in context.

Simply stated, it appears that vocabulary is primarily 'self-selected' and acquired when the situation is *compelling* enough to warrant the selection. Accordingly, it would then behoove the classroom teacher to deploy methods and activities that would create a degree of 'urgency' or 'immediacy' in the classroom. How might this be done? By way of example, I would like to offer the following activity to you.

***Function*-al Rap Activity**

It is conjectured that, at one time in human history, music and communication were one and the same; much like birdsong. Some linguists feel that Chinese, a highly intonal language known for its 'musicality', is one of the last remaining vestiges of this phenomenon in today's world. At some point, due to natural selection, music diverged from primary communication into a separate genre. (*I would conjecture that 'romance' probably had a lot to do with it...)*

The following activity is designed to fuse language acquisition and music together once again. 'Raps' are to be created by students based around specific language tasks, also known as 'functions'. Certain expressions and vocabulary words, selected for their applicability to the function, are provided to help them compose the lyrics.

STEP 1: Acquire the music.

This step is critical to the set up of the activity. Original rap background instrumentals by contemporary artists, without the controversial lyrics, are available for purchase online at various music download sites. *(Please note that we are working to acquire original background instrumentals, not re-recorded backgrounds done by other artists. Students do not take well to elevator music.)*

The music download site will have a search engine available. Simply type in 'rap instrumentals', hit enter and the download of background instrumentals will begin. The offerings will be varied and spread among several recording artists. If you are partial to a particular artist, type in 'rap instrumentals' followed by the artist's name and the download will be restricted to backgrounds associated with that artist.

STEP 2: Select the music.

I suggest that you vary the backgrounds based on beat and speed. Although you will have many to select from, I suggest that you limit your selection to no more than 10 songs. This number will provide you with variety. Then, pay the relatively minor expense for the music.

STEP 3: Provide the music to the students.

There are any number of ways to do this, but the easiest and most cost effective is to send the audio files to your students electronically. If you are not quite setting the world on fire technologically, simply ask one of your kids for help.

STEP 4: Organize the task.

- Now that everyone has music, it is time to set to the task. The first homework assignment is a simple one. Ask students to listen to the background instrumentals and to rank their top 3 favorites.

- The next day, divide your class into groups of 4 to 5 participants per group based on their preference ranking of the background instrumentals. When the first choice cannot be accommodated, move to the second or third choice.
- Arrange to have devices, such as the iPod (with portable speakers) available for each group. Most students have this equipment readily available. *(Some are now growing these devices as natural appendages!)*
- Advise the students of the following:
  - A rap will be written and eventually performed by each group.
  - The rap will be of a specific length. *(Initially, 3 stanzas of 4 lines each or 12 lines of lyrics is the recommendation.)*
  - The rap will focus on a specific linguistic function or task, chosen by the teacher, such as 'describing and discussing members of your family'.
  - Certain vocabulary words, idiomatic expressions and grammatical items will be provided by the teacher as prompts. However, the students may <u>not</u> use these words *exclusively* in building their raps.

Have the students turn on the music and begin the process. And, yes… As the groups will be playing various instrumentals, it will definitely have the feel of anarchy at first. This, however, is the sound of 'acquisition'. It is probably a good idea to close the door to your classroom before someone from the Math department closes it for you…

Depending on your situation, the activity may be spread out over weeks and need not be done every day. Figure 10 will serve as a rubric for implementation:

Linguistic Function: *Describing and discussing family members*

Helpful Vocabulary:

- la familia
- el abuelito
- el gato
- los ojos
- los lentes
- castaño
- alto
- el tío
- callado
- dormir

Helpful Expressions:

- cuenta chistes
- a mi lado
- de color café
- un poco alto
- conmigo

Sample Rap: *(Written by John De Mado)*
En mi familia somos cinco:
mi mamá, papá y yo,
el abuelito y tía María,
el perro Tico, el gato Limón.

Mi mamá tiene los ojos azules,
el pelo negro y usa lentes también.
Mi papá es un poco alto, con el pelo castaño,
es delgado y se viste muy bien.

Mi tía María es muy bonita,
con los ojos de color café.
El abuelito es gracioso, con el pelo canoso,
cuenta chistes, duerme hasta las diez.

El gato Limón es muy callado,
sólo quiere jugar y dormir.
Mi perro siempre está mi lado,
y conmigo él quiere salir.

Figure 10

STEP 5: Perform the raps.

As recommended by ACTFL, activities should be performance-based. Accordingly, when ample time has been given to creation of the raps and to practice of the respective performances (this includes not only the vocal piece but any choreography as well), each group will be assigned a particular date upon which to perform its rap. Hip-Hop gear should be encouraged. Although grades may be given, it is recommended that initially this not be done. Extra credit might be more appropriate.

Chapter 9

Vocabulary Acquisition and Content Literacy

My work with both public and independent schools around the United States has revealed a pervasive concern for declining literacy rates among students. Schools are channeling large sums of money into the remediation of reading and writing. Results from high stakes testing, such as state mastery tests, along with other national exams, are fueling the concern.

Much more emphasis appears to be placed upon reading than writing. It seems that our society is more forgiving of those who don't write well. Reading, however, is another story.

Historically, the teaching of reading has been assigned to the generalist primary/elementary school teacher. Yet, as we approach middle school and high school, the discipline largely falls to the English/Language Arts department.

The contemporary wisdom among those that teach reading underscores the belief that the more one reads, the more literate one becomes. This does sound logical and it is, to some degree, true; particularly if the reader is already 'literate'.

However, as a teacher of languages other than English, my experience points out that just because a child has mastered the sound/symbol relationships of a given language, this does not necessarily qualify him/her as being 'literate'. Time and time again, I have had students who were able read (decode) beautifully out loud in Spanish or French. Yet, when asked what they understood, the answer was often the same… "Not much…"

Is there another path to literacy that we might be overlooking?

As this chapter will be focusing on a discussion of 'literacy, it might be advantageous at this juncture to offer up a dictionary definition of the term.

According to Webster's Dictionary, literacy is defined as being 'the quality or state of being literate.' As this offers little by way of definition, one might be further compelled to explore the word 'literate', which carries a threefold definition:

- Educated, cultured
- Able to read and write
- Having knowledge and competence

The first of the three definitions is squarely rooted in the disciplines of Sociology and Sociolinguistics, implying that the extent of one's language skills and the way one deploys language has a great deal to do with how one is viewed by others.

The second is the schoolhouse definition; one which has not varied for centuries. One is literate when one reads and writes. This would imply, of course, that there are various levels of literacy, predicated upon just how well one reads or writes.

The last of the three posits a view that is quite expansive of nature; one that is more in sync with the definition of 'intelligence' offered up by developmental psychologist Howard Gardner. *My personal belief is that the words 'literacy' and 'intelligence' (as defined by Gardner) might be used interchangeably.*

Gardner's definition:

- Intelligence is observable.
- Intelligence is deployed to solve problems.
- Intelligence is used to create things of value within one's culture and across cultures.

Although this writer is predisposed to expanding boundaries in order to be legitimately more inclusive, this book is primarily focused on the schoolhouse and language acquisition. Thus, we will focus our discussion regarding literacy on definition number 2... *Able to read and write.*

In particular, we will discuss reading.

The National Reading Panel (NRP) has identified 5 components inherent to the acquisition of the reading skill:

- Phonemic Awareness
- Phonics
- Fluency
- Comprehension
- Vocabulary

Phonemic awareness occurs when the novice reader understands that 'spoken words are composed of tiny sound segments or *phonemes*.'

Phonics creates the reader's ability to 'link sounds to letter symbols and combine them to make words.'

Fluency encourages 'reading with speed, accuracy and proper expression without conscious attention; performing multiple reading tasks, such as *word recognition* and *comprehension*, at the same time.'

Comprehension seeks 'understanding, both explicitly and implicitly, of what is read.'

Vocabulary is fundamental to the reader's successful comprehension of what is being read.

There is no doubt that the first two components, phonemic awareness and phonics, are pivotal to the decoding process. Decoding simply means the ability to look at words written on a page and to say them correctly to yourself or out loud. It does not, however, guarantee comprehension.

Fluency, the third component, is an interesting word. Multilinguals are often asked whether they are 'fluent' in their non-native language(s). In actuality, fluency has less to do with the amount of language that one owns than the ability to produce that language seamlessly, with limited, if any, hesitation. Stutterers, while attending speech pathology sessions, are often asked to read out loud as part of the therapy. The speech therapist normally proceeds by listening carefully and noting the number of 'disfluencies' exhibited by the stutterer. Disfluencies are defined as words that are attacked inappropriately or that emerge from the reader in a less than facile fashion. In fact, most disfluencies are words that are part of the stutterer's active vocabulary and which can be decoded by the stutterer. He/she simply has difficulty producing them orally.

The assumption put forth by the NRP is that students that read quickly and with ease (fluently) will more likely be avid readers. I do believe that there is truth in that position. Yet, it is important to note that the speed with which one reads is, in many cases, dictated by the task at hand. Moreover, although the NRP is advocating a push for faster, more fluent reading in the schoolhouse, the reality is that most reading done there is for purposes that demand moderately slow to very slow rates of reading (*). To wit, Figure 11:

Reading and Rates

Type	Rate	Purpose
Scanning	Very fast	Quickly find specific details
Preview/Survey	Fast	Acquire general sense
Recreation	Moderate	Enjoyment
Critical*	Mod. Slow	Personal Reaction
Study*	Slow	Remember information
Analytical*	Very Slow	Get every detail

Figure 11

The final two components, vocabulary and comprehension are of greater importance to me. Above and beyond anything, the purpose for reading is to comprehend. It would appear to me that once one is capable of decoding the sound/symbol system of a given language, it is comprehension that determines whether one is a 'literate' reader or not and it is vocabulary that is fundamental to comprehension.

Previously, I posited the following question: *Is there another path to literacy that we might be overlooking?* I would like to address this question at this point and base my perspective on research from the University of Iowa, the researchers being Dr. Jerry Zimmerman and Dr. Carolyn Brown.

Literacy begins with the ears (listening), as well as the eyes (reading/viewing). Both are 'receptive' skills, with speaking and writing being the 'productive' skills. More specifically, literacy is a byproduct of 'comprehensible input'. According to Dr. Stephen Krashen, Professor Emeritus from the University of Southern California:

- Comprehensible input is central to language acquisition.
- We acquire language when we understand what is said, viewed and/or read.
- How it is said and written is inconsequential.
- Comprehensible input is central to literacy.
- We initially acquire language from 'comprehensible input' (listening/viewing/reading).

He further elaborates by saying:

- Comprehended input (intake) is what counts, not just input that is *potentially* comprehensible.
- Comprehensible input should also contain language that has not yet been acquired but which the learner is ready to acquire (i + 1).
- The more comprehensible input is provided, the more language acquisition and literacy is developed.

What is salient is the tacit inclusion of listening as a co-equal with reading as primary sources of literacy. My own belief is that listening has been downplayed in favor of reading to the detriment of literacy in general. I believe that people 'select' the language they end up owning; that they aggressively acquire specific language based on the situations in which they have found themselves and the problems they have had to resolve. Furthermore, I believe that none of us has one word in our lexicon that is not self-selected and that the words that we own are largely garnered from *conversation* rather than reading. Figure 12 offers a graphic of the march toward literacy.

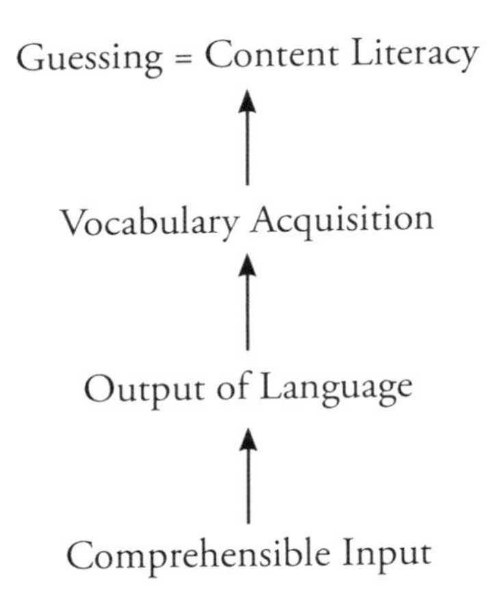

Figure 12

- At the base of literacy is Comprehensible Input. This is input that is understood by individuals when language is directed toward them
- When one understands what another is saying, this generally leads to output of language.
- When input and output of language are a consequence of one another, this is commonly known as *conversation.*
- Conversation is a major, if not primary source for garnering vocabulary.
- Language is ambiguous and thus inadequate for human needs.

- As a result, when we listen, read or view, we guess at the meaning of the message being delivered.
- Because language is, of nature, ambiguous, successful (literate) readers rely upon guessing as they seek comprehension.
- Vocabulary is what allows readers to guess successfully at meaning.
- The most iterate among us are the best guessers.

To achieve effective communication, whether in the second language classroom or in life in general, two conditions must exist:

1. The individual who is producing the language must attempt to make him/herself understood by delivering the message with 'comprehensible input' in mind; i.e., by doing everything possible to facilitate comprehension on the part of the listener. This includes hand gestures, facial expressions, body language, illustrations, music, etc.
2. The individual listening to the message must actively seek comprehensible input.

Imagine that the following passage is being delivered orally in Spanish at native speed with no attempt at comprehensible input. Spanish speakers will understand it and will chuckle at the subsequent moral. Those who don't speak Spanish, yet who actively seek to understand might look for cognates. Nonetheless, they will largely miss the message.

> *Había una vez una mamá ratoncita. La ratoncita vivía debajo de una casa… Con sus tres niños, Manny, Mo, y Jack. Un día, la familia decidió salir de debajo de la casa. ¿…Y qué vieron? ¡Vieron al gato! ¡Y todos tenían MUCHO miedo! Entonces, la mamá ratoncita tuvo una idea MUY buena… ¡Ella empezó a LADRAR! ¡Guau! ¡Guau! El gato tenía miedo y se escapó… Entonces, la mamá ratoncita les dijo a sus niños "Niños… ¡Una lección! ¡Es muy importante ser bilingüe!"*

Consider the same story delivered with a mild attempt at comprehensible input (visuals). If you are a non-Spanish speaker, did you understand more this time? Input is not the same as 'comprehensible input'.

Una Lección

Había una vez una mamá ratoncita...

La ratoncita vivía debajo de una casa...

Con sus tres niños... Manny, Mo y Jack...

Un día, la familia decidió salir de debajo de la casa.

¿Y que vieron?

¡Vieron al gato!

¡Y todos tenian MUCHO miedo!

Entonces, la mamá ratoncita tuvo una idea muy buena!

¡Ella empezó a LADRAR!

¡El gato tenía miedo y se escapó!

As previously stated, successful (literate) readers rely upon guessing as they seek comprehension and vocabulary is what allows them to guess successfully for meaning. I would like to elaborate by offering you two short passages to read. Please consider both by reading them aloud:

~ On Ltericay ~

Aoccdrnig to rscheearch at Cmabrigde Uinervtisy, it deosn't mttaer in waht odrer the ltteers in a wrod are. The olny iprmoetnt thnig is that the frist and lsat ltteer be at the rghit pclae. The rset can be a tatol mses. Yet, you can slitl raed it wouthit a porbelm. Tihs is bcuseae the hamun mind deos not raed ervey lteter istlef, but rahter the wrod as a wlohe... (Amzaning, dno't you tnihk?)

How did you do? Were you able to comprehend the passage successfully despite the linguistic interference? I anticipate that you were probably successful in your attempt to decode the first of the two passages. Now, I invite you to read a related passage:

Niotcais

Sgeun un etsduio de una uivenrsdiad ignlsea, no ipmotra el odren en el que las ltears están ersciats. La uicna csoa ipormnate es que la pmrirea y la utlima ltera estén escritas en la psiocion cocrrtea. El rsteo peude estar ttaolmntee mal y aun pordas leerlo sin pobrleams. Esto es pquore no lemeos cada ltera por si msima, snio la palabra en un todo. Presnoamelnte, me preace icrneilbe.

Were you successful with the second passage? Perhaps. Perhaps not. It would be easy to contend that your inability to read passage number two is due to the fact that you simply do not speak Spanish. However, just as passage number one is not English, passage number two is not Spanish.

I would expand upon that statement by saying that should there have been a comprehension problem with passage number 2, it is really due to a lack of vocabulary, and because of that deficit, you are unable to guess at the meaning. If, by some odd chance, you owned only the 68 reminiscent Spanish words that comprise passage number two and no other Spanish vocabulary, you would be able to guess at the meaning and therefore successfully comprehend. An excerpt from the classic Lewis Carroll poem, The Jabberwocky, illustrates a similar point:

And, as in uffish thought he stood,
The Jabberwock, with eyes of flame,
Came whiffling through the tulgey wood,
And burbled as it came!

One, two! One, two! And through and through
The vorpal blade went snicker-snack!
He left it dead, and with its head
He went galumphing back.

"And, hast thou slain the Jabberwock?
Come to my arms, my beamish boy!
O frabjous day! Callooh! Callay!'
He chortled in his joy.

Although certain words inherent to this piece are clearly not found in an English dictionary, the reader can guess at meaning as a result of prior lexical, grammatical and syntactical knowledge. 'Uffish' must be describing 'thought' because it ends in 'ish', like so many other English adjectives. 'Whiffling' must come from 'to whiffle', an action word, because it ends in 'ing' just as 'galumphing' must come from 'to galumph'. 'Tulgey', ending in 'y' and preceding 'wood' probably describes said noun and gives us a sense nature and context. Although complete comprehension is not in the offing, acquaintance with English words, how they contribute to a phrase and their location in the phrase, can help us to guess for at least limited comprehension. ***Vocabulary, along with some grammatical and syntactical awareness, allows us to guess.***

Chapter 10

Language Acquisition, Culture and Viewing

Language without culture is Esperanto. Culture without language is travelogue. The trick is to find balance between the two in the language classroom. Is it possible to engage students in a cultural milieu that is other than their own while transmitting the language of instruction 90% of the time as recommended by ACTFL?

If used properly, film can be a great source of comprehensible input. As we have seen previously, comprehensible input is at the foundation of language acquisition and literacy.

By way of review, I offer the characteristics of comprehensible input once again:

- The language acquirer understands the input.
- Comprehended input (intake) is what counts, not just input that is *potentially* comprehensible.
- Comprehensible input should also contain language that has not yet been acquired but which the learner is ready to acquire (i + 1).
- The more comprehensible input is provided, the more language acquisition and literacy are developed.

Use of target language film in the language classroom often takes on a linear dimension, with viewing moving precipitously from beginning to end. English subtitles interrupt the L2 acquisition process and are often followed by factual, not interpretive questions formulated in English (sometimes justifiable as explained later) and arranged in chronological order. The result is a language experience devoid of risk-taking, vulnerability and intuition. I envision viewing to be something more circuitous, often doubling back on itself in order to challenge the viewer.

Reading and viewing require the same subset of skills due to the fact that both are 'receptive' in nature. Whether you are constructing meaning from the printed word or from the 'big screen', the way one views is impacted by one's purpose for viewing:

Viewing and Rates

Type	Rate	Purpose
Scanning	Very casual	Quickly find specific details
Preview/Survey	Casual	Acquire general sense
Recreation	Moderately casual	Enjoyment
Critical	Moderately intent	Personal Reaction
Study	Intent	Remember information
Analytical	Very intent	Absorb all details

Figure 13

Furthermore, just as with reading, the visual medium selected by the teacher should be commensurate to the age and viewing ability of the audience.

When it comes to reading, Stephen Krashen advises that there should be a gradual wade-in, almost like entering a swimming pool. Inexperienced swimmers are apt to enter the shallow end and, as their confidence increases, venture out into the deeper extremities of the pool. He states that target language comic books are a great starting point as they are of limited length, easy to carry, filled with contemporary vocabulary and supported by visuals (comprehensible input) at every turn. He suggests moving to magazines next for all the same reasons but with the added benefit of topical variety ranging from fashion, to pop culture, to sports and beyond. Newspapers are the subsequent choice to follow magazines with adolescent novels culminating the process.

To parallel Krashen's thinking on wade-in, I would like to offer the following suggestions regarding viewing in general. Begin with target language animations moving over time to game shows, reality shows and soap operas. News broadcasts would logically follow, approximating the reading of newspapers. Full-length target language films would complete the process.

To further relate to the skill of reading, effective viewing requires 3 stages as well:

- BEFORE VIEWING
- VIEWING
- AFTER VIEWING

BEFORE VIEWING: This is the stage that allows students to *anticipate meaning* and to guess freely, without consequence, at what might happen in the story line of the visual media. Viewers are encouraged to make global predictions and to take risks, be vulnerable and to use their intuition. The goal is to seek 'comprehensible input' by activating prior knowledge.

Quite often 'out takes' or 'trailers' for the film are available as 'special features' on a DVD. As a first step before viewing the film itself, an effective way to encourage language students to anticipate meaning and to make global predictions is to have them view these 'special feature' segments without sound or subtitles. Students should be directed to 'predict' the eventual story line of the film using their intuition. Depending on student L2 proficiency levels, this may be accomplished in English. Remember that we are only trying to establish their level of acquaintance with the topic. Advise that they should consider gestures, facial expressions and context to aid their guessing. Each 'special feature' should be carefully segmented to aid recall.

A student organizer similar to the one in Figure 14 might serve to facilitate the task at hand:

BEFORE VIEWING ORGANIZER

- Title of Film:
- Type of Film (adventure, romance, etc.):
- General Topic or Theme:
- My Purpose for Viewing (based on Figure 13):
- What I Know about the Topic:
- What I Expect to See and Hear:

Figure 14

Assuming that someone will make a somewhat accurate guess about the content he or she has viewed initially, it is recommended that the teacher pose a series of straightforward recognition questions to assess student background regarding the topic. To wit:

- What do you think is happening here?
- Have you ever done this yourself?
- Have you ever been there or somewhere similar?
- How would you have reacted?
- Do you know someone in a similar situation? How so?

'Recognition' activities seek to assess what information the language learner has gathered from the stimuli. As these are 'recognition' questions designed to ascertain comprehension, it is legitimate and linguistically sound to avoid confusing linguistic tasks by posing the questions in English, particularly at the novitiate levels. *Nothing, including the target language, should impede the student from seeking comprehensible input.* Teachers should provide multiple and varied opportunities for their students to demonstrate recognition.

Step 2 might be to view the media without sound, but with target language subtitles. This provides an opportunity to look for English cognates. The organizer may be employed again to allow students to revise their guesses.

Step 3 might ask students to view the media with both sound and subtitles.

Step 4 might require viewing with sound but without subtitles. The organizer may be used with each step, encouraging revision and reconsideration.

VIEWING: The goal of this stage is to *construct meaning*. Now that students have activated prior knowledge, anticipated meaning and sought comprehensible input, it is time to view the actual film. It is important that the viewing be done in manageable segments with logical breaks. Once students have had a chance to make an initial pass at viewing a specific segment of the film, they are asked once again to assess and revise the predictions made in the 'Before Viewing' stage. Unlike that stage, however, the classroom teacher discretely monitors comprehension at various checkpoints by posing specific recognition questions pertaining to content, such as:

- In what country do you think this film takes place?
- What does the man in the uniform do for a living?
- What does the bicycle imply to you?
- What type of village is this? How do the people earn a living? What makes you think that?
- Is the young woman interested in the young man? How do you know?
- Is the man on the train famous? How do you know?
- Where does the young woman work?
- What emotion is being expressed by the elderly woman? Why do you think that? What might she be saying?

In this manner, one would proceed through the visual media, stopping strategically to check comprehension, whether through direct questioning or another form of recognition activity.

AFTER VIEWING: This final stage asks students to 'reconstruct' and 'extend' the meaning of the content viewed. As such, they are asked to summarize, then retell and finally evaluate the film. It might be best to replay the movie trailer, should there be one available on the DVD, in order to aid student recall. Generally, the trailer acts as a brief synopsis of the entire story line.

A teacher may ask for 'summarization' at various culminating points during the viewing process. Below, please find an activity designed to encourage summarization.

- *Draw five pictures, in chronological order, that describe the scene that you have just viewed.*
- *Write a sentence or two under each one in the target language that relates what is happening.*
- *Share your drawings with a partner and explain their content to her/him in the target language.*

There is a difference between 'summarizing' the story and 'retelling' the story. Of nature, summaries are brief narratives focusing on a specific 'internal' segment, interlude or event in a broader overall story. 'Retelling' involves relating a larger story. Although this may imply the entire story line from beginning to end, it can also include complete scenes. The following is an example of a simple activity to encourage retelling:

> *Imagine that, over the weekend, you have viewed our film in a movie theater. Back in school on Monday, a classmate asks what you did on Saturday. When you say that you went to the movies, he/she wants to know what you saw and if there were any good scenes. Using the film that we are viewing in class, select a scene that you particularly enjoyed and retell what happened.*

The 'summarizing' and 'retelling' stages broadly ask the student to recount the story line verbatim, in segments that may be smaller or larger, depending on which task the student has been asked to undertake.

The 'evaluation' stage largely encourages students to 'extend' their learning by offering and supporting personal opinions pertaining to what has been viewed. This, of course, requires not only discrete knowledge regarding the film or animation, but also maximal ability to risk-take, be vulnerable and to use intuition. Of nature, activities that 'extend' the learning are open-ended and normally do not seek any specific correct response. To wit:

As a movie critic, your job is to comment on an actor's performance. In the context of the scene that you have just watched, comment on the performances of the two respective actors.

It is important to remember that successful viewing is not a passive activity. It requires engagement on the student's part. As such, I offer the following general suggestions to encourage student involvement:

- Require that students keep a viewing log. They should note not only the chronology of events but their reaction to those events as well.
- As the viewing log is an informal document, expect marginal notes, erasures, and less than perfect prose.
- Remind students to focus on targeted viewing strategies such as scanning, previewing, surveying, etc. and to be aware of the link between the purpose for viewing and the rate of viewing.
- Provide critical thinking questions for students as well as discrete factual questions.
- Ask students to construct imagined interviews with the director or actor.
- Use student-developed multiple-choice quizzes.
- Ask students to retell the story frequently.

Chapter 11

The Principled Approach (TPA)

There is a distinct difference between an 'approach' and a 'method'. An approach is philosophical in nature and pertains to a teacher's belief system or, as written in Alice Omaggio Hadley's Teaching Language in Context, a teacher's organizing principles. Conversely, a method reflects the arsenal of instructional techniques that a teacher deploys to implement that belief system or those organizing principles.

ACTFL (The American Council on the Teaching of Foreign Languages) has recurrently reminded us that, for a language department to be successful, it must be philosophically cohesive to the greatest degree possible. What exactly does that mean?... Does that imply that all members of a department must teach the same way?... If so, is that actually a realistic expectation?...

I have consulted with language departments in every state in the USA as well as with a number abroad. One thing that I have found to be indisputable is the fact that, of nature, we language teachers are a very independent lot. We are collegial to one another up to a point; that point of separation pertaining to the methods that we employ and deploy on a daily basis. We are very deferential to one another when the topic arises. It is, I suppose, professional courtesy. Yet, it may be just that deference that is deterring us from our stated mission of delivering to the USA, and thus to the world, a generation of American born students who can function in at least one other language.

Moreover, is it realistic to actually expect each language teacher in a given language department to teach the same way? I am inclined to say no. The way one teaches is influenced by several factors: beliefs held, experience, willingness to experiment, age, tethering to the textbook, departmental or district exams, personality, etc. It is best not to guess at such matters, but rather to gather the requisite empirical evidence. Accordingly, I have interviewed literally thousands of teachers over the years and virtually all of them admit to some level of instructional dissonance within their respective language departments. Below, you will find an inventory that I customarily use when surveying language teachers about their belief systems (Figure 15). The amount of divergence in response is amazing, not only among those who answer 'yes' or 'no', but among those who simply 'do not know'.

BELIEFS SURVEY

Please respond based on what you truly believe:

1. STUDENTS ACQUIRE LANGUAGE AT THE SAME RATE. ___YES ___NO
2. A STUDENT, IN L2, CAN EXCEED HIS/HER ABILITY IN THE NATIVE TONGUE (L1). ___YES ___NO
3. LINGUISTIC ERRORS ARE LARGELY NEGATIVE AND LEAD TO 'FOSSILIZATION' OF THE ERRORS. ___YES ___NO
4. *ALL* STUDENTS ARE 'CANDIDATES' TO BE MULTILINGUAL. ___YES ___NO
5. LANGUAGES CAN BE 'MASTERED'. ___YES ___NO
6. LANGUAGES ARE PRIMARILY LEARNED THROUGH IMITATION. ___YES ___NO
7. ACCURACY IS MORE IMPORTANT THAN LINGUISTIC INVENTIVENESS. ___YES ___NO
8. LANGUAGE IS ONLY 'STANDARD' WHEN GRAMMATICALLY ACCURATE. ___YES ___NO
9. GRAMMAR CREATES COMMUNICATION. ___YES ___NO
10. LANGUAGES CAN BE TAUGHT. ___YES ___NO

Figure 15

The Principled Approach (TPA)

It appears that there is a philosophical line drawn in the sand between those who consider themselves to be 'Proficiency-oriented' and those that consider themselves more 'traditional'. In reality, the flashpoint between the two factions is 'grammar and syntax'. Teachers that tend to be more traditional feel that language acquisition is a byproduct of sound grammatical instruction coupled with a keen eye toward accuracy. They generally hold the belief that Proficiency-oriented teachers essentially neglect accuracy and grammar. Conversely, Proficiency-oriented teachers are apt to believe that more traditional language teachers have little to no interest in communication skills other than reading and writing in the target language.

This debate is a waste of time and passion and does not serve to advance our agenda. The question does not revolve around whether grammar and syntax should be taught. *Structure and syntax are natural consequences of language acquisition.* There are no languages devoid of a structural and syntactical code. Rather, the real issue is 'why'?... Why is it important to provide grammatical and syntactical instruction? To my way of thinking, the importance of structural and syntactical accuracy is not in the creation of communication per se, but rather in the avoidance of miscommunication.

Which all leads me to these reflections: *As language teachers, where might we find common ground?... What can we actually agree on?... How might we develop, to the greatest extent possible, more philosophically cohesive language departments?... How do we minimize instructional dissonance?... Is methodology the answer?... Do we need to be more reflective in our instruction?*

I believe that the answers to the preceding questions cannot be solved through 'methodology'. As previously stated, there simply is too much instructional diversity within a given language department to achieve the cohesiveness required for success. However, there is something that predates methods. That something is called the 'organizing principle'.... And it is the foundation of ***The Principled Approach (TPA).***

Historically, we have seen many methodological trends come and go. And, in reality, there is a grain of truth in all of them. As a result, most of us that labor in the linguistic vineyard tend to be eclectic in our teaching strategies, favoring a blend of methods over strict allegiance to one specific methodology. I believe that those of us who enjoy a long tenure in our profession, and have tried most everything methodologically, will admit that there is no *'silver bullet'*... No one methodology that delivers it all.

An 'organizing principle' is the foundation of any belief system. It is so compelling in nature that it can be ignored neither in life nor in one's instruction. It is certifiably true by virtue of research and experience and not simply a byproduct of one's opinion. It helps us to know when we are misdirected in our efforts and when to recalibrate. It helps us to perceive when what we are doing is effective and why. In short, it is our instructional 'North Star'.

My personal journey as a World Language teacher, author and consultant has led me to many awakenings regarding language acquisition; i.e. how the human mind creates and acquires language. My beliefs, my 'organizing principles', have been hard earned through classroom experience, reading mountains of research, maintaining a willingness to admit that there was much that I didn't know and having a healthy respect for the benefits of risk-taking. I have always found the following quote by George F. Kneller to be a source of inspiration and reflection:

> *"Human beings who wish to become authentic persons must take their chances and be prepared for consequences. In the Socratic sense, you must begin to know by not knowing. If you know that you do not know, you may be born again. But you will not be born again without the pain of birth. And you will have to do violence to your soul... to make it live."*

George F. Kneller
Existentialism and Education
Philosophical Library, 1958
New York, New York

The Principled Approach (TPA)

Simply stated, ***The Principled Approach (TPA)*** invites language departments not to agree on methods necessarily, but rather forge unanimity of beliefs. It invites language departments to establish common ground by creating their own set of 'organizing principles'. These are not opinion statements, but rather statements of beliefs rooted in research, particularly pertaining to Applied Linguistics. They are intelligent affirmations that clearly and succinctly state what the department believes about language acquisition.

In essence, once a given language department can agree philosophically, it makes no difference what methods are employed, as long as those methods support and eventually deliver the departmental organizing principles. *"All roads lead to Rome..."*

Neither do I expect nor do I seek your immediate concurrence. After all, my organizing principles are a byproduct of my own research and reflection. You may not thoroughly understand the meaning of some based on the word tracks that I have selected. But believe me when I tell you that, should you ask for clarification, I can explain each one succinctly and with enthusiasm... And yes, I can quote the research.

To appreciate the impact that organizing principles have upon methodology, I would like to provide an example. Consider one of my personal organizing principles:

People who communicate take risks. There is an intimate relationship between language acquisition and the amount of risk-taking, vulnerability and intuition encouraged.

Linguistic risk-taking refers to the willingness of a language acquirer to confront more language than what she/he owns. Vulnerability means a willingness to err for the broader goal of communication. Intuition refers to the ability to skim and scan for information. I believe that these are primordial psycholinguistic characteristics that need to be carefully nurtured in students. I believe that the classroom needs to reinforce the development of these characteristics in students. I believe that teachers need to exhibit these characteristics themselves to the greatest degree possible.

If you were to fully embrace the aforementioned principle, as I do, how might this impact your instruction or the methods that you employ?… I would venture a guess that your classroom would focus more on situations and dramatizations and less on lecture. It probably would include problems to be resolved using the target language; i.e. asking someone out on a date. I would imagine that your tolerance for error would increase exponentially, thus changing your rubrics, assessments and grading habits. There would be greater emphasis on vocabulary acquisition and a reduced emphasis on grammar and syntactical instruction. Your role would evolve from being the 'editor' in the classroom to that of the 'Applied Linguist', steadfastly seeking to understand how the human mind actually creates and acquires language. The classroom would be more student-centered and less teacher-centered, allowing for more faith in the language acquisition process and, thus, in the language acquirer.

The amount that this would occur and the methods employed would, of course, vary from teacher to teacher. The important point, once again, is that there is concurrence on the organizing principle(s). The methods are secondary.

I want more American students to function in other languages. Our traditional hyper focus on methodology has not delivered the goods, despite our sincere intentions. We talk about the need for teachers to be more 'reflective' in their instruction. Well… Here is the opportunity. I believe that ***The Principled Approach' (TPA)*** can lead us to our stated goal of multilingualism for our students and to a more fulfilling professional life for those of us tasked with that goal.

What do we have to lose?…

Chapter 12

Organizing Principles

10 Organizing Principles for Language Acquisition

1. There is an intimate relationship between language acquisition and the amount of risk-taking, vulnerability and intuition encouraged by the teacher and exhibited by the acquirer.
2. Language transfer may be the single most common strategy deployed by language acquirers.
3. 'Error' (linguistic interference) is a byproduct of language transfer.
4. An 'error' is not the same as a 'mistake'.
5. In the language acquisition process, error is best viewed as a positive, not a negative.
6. For all intents and purposes, 'absolute bilingualism' is unattainable.
7. Language teachers are responsible for a minimum of 3 languages in the classroom: L1, L2 and 'Interlanguage'.
8. Language moves from 'non-standard' toward 'standard', with or without instructional intervention.
9. Concerns over 'fossilization' should be minimized.
10. 'Interlingualism' really is our instructional target.

10 Organizing Principles for Inclusion

1. A child who functions in one language is already a candidate to function in others.
2. Tolerating a student in class is not the same as including the student.
3. There are many types of language users.
4. Language, of nature, is inclusionary.
5. IQ is not a prerequisite for effective second language acquisition.
6. Most of what is exclusionary about second language acquisition revolves around the issue of accuracy.
7. There are many paths to cognition.
8. People who communicate take risks, are willing to be vulnerable and use intuition.
9. An inclusionary approach to second language acquisition must be supported by inclusionary assessment.
10. Inclusionary assessment must be supported by inclusionary grading strategies.

10 Organizing Principles for Language Acquisition and Literacy

1. Language acquisition begins with 'comprehensible input'.
2. Comprehensible input encourages 'output' of language, thus encouraging conversation.
3. Most of the vocabulary we own comes from broad conversation, ***not reading***, and is self-selected.
4. The amount of vocabulary we own ultimately determines 'literacy'.
5. Language is ambiguous and often inadequate for human needs.
6. Successful reading is ultimately determined by comprehension of what is read, not simply ***decoding***.
7. Due to the ambiguity of language, we 'guess' when we listen, read and view.
8. Vocabulary enables us to 'guess' when we listen, read and view.
9. Abundant vocabulary enhances our ability to 'guess' effectively.
10. The most literate among us are the best 'guessers'.

10 Organizing Principles for Language Acquisition and Viewing

1. Viewing requires a gradual wade-in, moving from target language animations to games shows, reality shows and soap operas, then to news broadcasts and finally to full length target language films.
2. In order for viewing to turn into successful language acquisition, 3 stages must be accommodated:
   Before Viewing, Viewing and After Viewing.
3. Before Viewing allows students to activate prior knowledge, anticipate meaning, risk-take and to seek comprehensible input, the foundation of language acquisition.
4. Viewing allows students to *construct meaning* through periodic comprehension check-points
5. After Viewing activities allow students to *reconstruct* and *extend* meaning through *summarization, retelling and evaluation* of the story line.
6. Viewing is not a passive activity.
7. Comprehensible input (CI) is at the foundation of language acquisition and literacy.
8. Film and animation are prime sources of CI.
9. The visual media must be commensurate to the age and viewing ability of the audience.
10. Viewing is a receptive skill and, as such, is subject to type, rate and purpose.

Epilogue

A Profession in Search of Language

We are truly a profession in search of language...

Most American World Language teachers are well tenured. Methodologically, they have witnessed, as well as survived, the grammar translation method, direct method, the onset of the audio-lingual materials, labored with the notional-functional syllabus and strained to understand the ever elusive 'Proficiency' orientation.

Based upon my frequent interactions with language teachers around the nation, it becomes increasingly evident that what impedes us from implementing our desire to render a generation of 'homegrown' multilingual students to our nation is our historic preparation.

Most of us have been amply trained with regard to methodology; that is, how the teacher teaches. Very few of us, including the newly arrived to our profession, have a fuller notion of language acquisition theory; that is, how the human mind actually creates and acquires language. We are armed with an arsenal of teaching techniques that often miss their mark largely because we don't understand the nature of the target that we seek.

Engaged language departments around the nation are turning to the research as a catalyst for change. Professional and staff development workshops, heretofore focused primarily upon "teaching tips", now emphasize the language acquisition process and how to replicate it in the schoolhouse to the greatest degree possible. At the foundation of these workshops exists one overriding premise:

Teaching will never suffice for what 'acquisition' must accomplish...